Blessing Mistakes

Learn to give yourself and others Grace, not grief, when a mistake is made.

YOU MATTER
MORE THAN
THE MISTAKE

Brenda Miller
Bestselling author of *The Kid Code,*
30 Second Parenting Strategies

"I absolutely love your work—you are providing really powerful and practical techniques for parents."

—Jack Canfield,
Bestselling Co-Author of Chicken Soup for the Soul Series

BALBOA.PRESS
A DIVISION OF HAY HOUSE

Balboa Press books may be ordered through booksellers or by contacting:

Balboa Press
A Division of Hay House
1663 Liberty Drive
Bloomington, IN 47403
www.balboapress.com
844-682-1282

Print information available on the last page.

ISBN: 978-1-9822-7557-0 (sc)
ISBN: 978-1-9822-7558-7 (e)

Balboa Press rev. date: 10/15/2021

Dedicated to my husband, Blake,
who has so graciously blessed
my (many) mistakes.

CONTENTS

Be a Part of the Blessing Mistakes Movement

– Teach this act of kindness to your family by making it the go-to in your house when a mistake is made. Say and feel the truth of this statement: "You matter so much more than the mistake."
– Say and feel the truth of this statement to yourself when you make a mistake: "I matter more than the mistake." Then make the mistake right.
– Use it every day with every mistake.
– Every negative state is a mistake. Bless yourself or another for being in a negative state.
– Share this strategy for peace with your kids.
– As a reminder, place a sticky note on your fridge that says, "For love's sake, bless the mistake."
– To learn more about the Blessing Mistakes Movement, visit www.thekidcode.ca

Also Available for Your and Your Child's Well-Being

– *The Kid Code, 30 Second Parenting Strategies* has one hundred simple strategies to give parents and their kids "right now relief" in an upset, visit www.thekidcode.ca.
– To take a class on peaceful, positive parenting in the time it takes to have a coffee break, visit www.thekidcode.ca
– To become a Kid Code teacher and teach classes about Blessing Mistakes and many other strategies to get immediate relief in an upset: https://www.thekidcode.ca/become-a-kid-code-teacher
– The following courses are available at www.courserebel. com: Ending Upsets Instantly, Peace Practices, Becoming an Inhospitable Host to Addictions, Self-Healing, Attention Determines Your Destiny, Autism, and 21 Days to a Better Memory.

Coming Soon

- *Mr. Upalupagus's Secret Secrets*, a children's bedtime, and a family anytime storybook that teaches the secrets of dissolving stress and uncovering our natural joy. It helps kids learn how to get back into their natural states when a challenge arises. Mr. Upalupagus's crew of a little bit rowdy but lovable animals go on adventures and learn something beautiful about their inner selves! This book follows the principles taught in *The Kid Code, 30 Second Parenting Strategies:* www.thekidcode.ca
- *BullyProof Yourself (And Your Kids)* is a how to stop being bullied from a conscious perspective. It's packed with self-inquiry exercises that help us stop attracting bullies into our lives, and help us meet and defeat the bully: www.thekidcode.ca

ACKNOWLEDGMENTS

Thanks to so many people for making this book a reality: My dad for teaching me this simple humanitarian, respectful, and connecting way of being in the world. My husband and kids for blessing my many mistakes. My grandkids for reminding me without knowing it that it's natural to be loving toward others when a mistake is made. Special thanks to my best friend, Lesia, who is my longtime 'inner-work buddy'. We've worked everything and anything that could stand in the way of our natural joy, and as a result, we've come into clarity and joy together. Thanks to the original group of Kid Code teachers: Amanda, Lasha, Tyla, Louise, Janna, Trista, and Julie, and to those who come after, for spreading this precious stress-reducing act of kindness to as many as possible. Thanks to all the extraordinary people at Balboa Press who helped this book get published and into your hands. And finally, thanks to you for making this a more peaceful world by using Blessing Mistakes.

CHAPTER 1

The Blessing of a Blessing: Grace Grows Us in One Direction, Grief in the Other

---

Grumpy or gracious
Pick one!

One day I was driving my dad's too-big truck in a too-small corral and put a dent in it. When I showed him and apologized, he opened his arms wide for me to walk in to for a hug and said, "It doesn't matter a particle." On that day I learned how to give myself and others grace, not grief, when a mistake is made.

> *The magic is in the message:*
>
> *"You matter more than the mistake."*

Making Life Easy

When things don't add up
in your life, start subtracting.
—Unknown

On that day I also learned what works well in relationships—and in life—when mistakes are made. I learned that we have the ability to show love to another person and ourselves when a mistake is made, even though we are often taught otherwise. When we show love to someone who has made a mistake, we both get to feel love. When we are decent to someone who has made a mistake, instead of feeling bad, the person feels safe and cherished. We develop respect and long-lasting connections when we show love to someone who has made a mistake. It feels natural to us to give each other Grace instead of grief, and when we do, we become more comfortable with ourselves and want to pass blessing mistakes on to other people to help them get relief when they make mistakes.

We don't feel any of those wonderful things if we give someone grief. We polish our hearts and deliver ourselves straight to our own well-being if we bring this simple but profound practice into our lives.

Since that day,
I've been looking
for a good reason
to give another person grief
and haven't found one.

I'm still looking.

From Panic to Peace

"I went from panicked to peaceful in a matter of seconds when I applied this simple strategy after spilling my coffee and later my morning smoothie all over the counter.

Blessing mistakes defuses upsets before they have a chance to derail you.

This strategy from *The Kid Code, 30Second Parenting Strategies* highlights the awareness that children and adults are so much more valuable than being defined by a mistake.

When a mishap happens and my son says to me, "Bless you, Mom. You matter more than a mistake," my heart melts, and so does the tension around the situation.

We quickly reset and move forward with the day.

Blessing Mistakes is a blessing!"

Julie Veresh
Innate Dynamics
Intuitive Coach
Kid Code Teacher

Who Can Use Blessing Mistakes?

If you do not sow in the spring,
you do not reap in the autumn.
—Unknown

- Parents
- Kids
- Extended family
- Grandparents
- Teachers
- Coaches
- Volunteers
- Anyone who wants to feel and spread peace.

Blessings or Blunders?

As you slide down the bannister of life,
may the splinters never point
the wrong way.
—Irish Blessing

The purpose of a blessing is to return us to our essential natures, aka our true selves, natural states, and True Natures. In these states we are joyful, compassionate, curious, inclusive, natural, genuine, creative, harmless, and wise beyond words. We know this to be true because in these states we *feel* natural. This truth is repeated several times throughout the book. Each time is an invitation to stop and become aware *of the truth* of the statement. This will help you take the understanding deeper and bring you closer to seeing when you are in, or out of your natural state.

> GRANDDAUGHTER: Grama why does blessing mistakes feel good?

> ME: Because if we understand that all people matter more than their mistakes and *feel* the truth of that statement, we return to our True Nature. Blessing mistakes points us to our natural states.

> GRANDDAUGHTER: Grama, did you write that down?

The Blessing of a Blessing

Counting your blessings
piles them up!

Blessing a mistake that you make, that your child makes, that any other human being makes, that an organization makes, that a corporation makes, or that a government makes means you don't have to deal with the damage you do to yourself when you devalue and belittle another human being or an organization. Giving others grief when they make mistakes damages you. To prove this to yourself, notice how you feel when you treat others cruelly versus how you feel when you bless someone's mistake. One steals your well-being, and the other promotes it.

When you bless mistakes, you can have more rewarding relationships. The other human being doesn't have to deal with the damage of being devalued and belittled. You support instead of oppress others, and that helps them and you. You don't have to cover up, deny, make excuses for, or justify your mistake and suffer the internal pain of those reactions. You get to admit it, bless yourself, and make it right. There is no residue, no footprint. You are left feeling free. You escape conditioning you don't even know is in your unconscious mind that is acting out against you and others.

Miracles in Relationships

"We all make mistakes but taking the time to pause and realize that they are simply mistakes and that they are part of life can bring so much freedom to you and those you around you.

It allows you the opportunity for grace and gratitude and creates miracles in all types of relationships.

Blessing mistakes is not just for kids; it is a technique that I use often in all areas of my life.

I use it with my nieces and nephews, other family, friends, my husband, my staff, and most importantly myself. It is so simple but profoundly powerful.

It heals the hearts of those you use it on. For example: When I have used this technique with my 4-year-old niece Maya, and my 2-year-old nephew Bentley, I see their little faces go from worry, sadness, and fear back to joy and beingness so quickly. It takes all the bad feelings away so fast!

When I have used this technique with my husband, it opens our hearts to each other and brings renewed joy and trust to the relationship in an instant.

When I use this technique with my staff, they are better at their jobs.

When I use this technique on myself, it builds my compassion for others and allows me to let myself off the hook so that I can move forward to problem solve the situation more easily.

It clears the way for peace. It truly is remarkable.

Blessing mistakes is something simple that we can implement in our lives that I believe will change the world for the good of all. I invite you to just try it today and see the instant healing and peace that can happen in your life!"

Trista Davis
Owner, Above Average Wellness,
Yoga and Meditation Instructor
Kid Code Teacher

What Is a Blessing?

Blessed is the opposite of stressed.

According to the *Oxford Advanced Dictionary*, a "blessing" is something that is "endowed with divine favor."

As defined by the Office 365 thesaurus, "blessing" has several meanings. A blessing can be an approval—to bless something is to esteem it, respect it, appreciate it, honor it, revere it, encourage it, and hold it in high regard. To bless something is to value it, prize it, cherish it, and hold it dear.

A blessing can be a miracle, a godsend, a boon, a lucky thing, a good thing, or a stroke of luck. It can be a consecration, a sanctification, an exalting, a hallowing, a benediction, or a sacred sign.

A blessing is when everything seems to work in your favor. You often feel like you have received good fortune. You feel grateful. You realize the "bad" stuff and all the upsets you experienced are also blessings because they wake you up to your beautiful True Nature. The awareness that life itself is a blessing makes its way into your consciousness, and you focus on that instead of on complaining and negativity, which don't feel good to you and create more of the same. You notice that when you are negative and complaining, you are driving yourself away from your own well-being.

Feeling blessed makes you want to share all your blessings.

What Is a Mistake?

I never make the same mistake twice.
I make it five or six times,
you know, just to be sure.
—Unknown

As defined by the Office 365 thesaurus, a mistake is an error, blunder, slipup, gaff, oversight, misstep, blooper, lapse, muddle, miscalculation, or faux pas.

A mistake is something you didn't want or mean to happen, but you are still responsible for, such as dropping something or making a mess; forgetting to do something; or being hurtful, mean, or displaying other awful behaviors. Lying, cheating, and stealing can also be mistakes. Give everyone in your family the benefit of the doubt; they must not really want to do those things. Bless them; it's easier on you, and they are still responsible for their actions.

Withholding Good Wishes

> *The love that you withhold*
> *is the pain that you carry.*
> —Ralph Waldo Emerson

In many parts of the world, as soon as someone sneezes, it is common to hear a word or statement of good wishes such as, "Bless you," or some version of, "To your health." It's natural to wish well-being to others.

We know this to be true because when we genuinely wish another well-being, we *feel* natural, and we *feel* well-being inside ourselves. If we can give good wishes when others sneeze, it seems humanitarian to offer good wishes when a mistake is made.

Giving Grief

You cannot do a kindness too soon,
for you never know how soon
it will be too late.
—Ralph Waldo Emerson

The following are examples of giving grief:

- Punishing ourselves or others.
- Feeling or expressing anger.
- Criticizing or judging ourselves or others.
- Belittling or humiliating ourselves or others.
- Embarrassing or shaming ourselves or someone else.
- Nagging at ourselves or others.
- Fighting with ourselves and others.
- Bullying ourselves or others.
- Causing ourselves or others trouble, unrest, upset, agitation, distress, anxiety.

We feel awful inside when we do any of those things.
If we do something that feels awful to us,
we're not caring for our well-being.
We're not in our natural state.

The Muddle of Mistakes

Making mistakes is better than faking perfection.
—Unknown

Ponder the muddle we make out of making mistakes.

Have you ever made a mistake?
How many every day?
How do you treat yourself when you make a mistake?
How do you feel when you treat yourself that way?
How do you treat others when they make mistakes?
How do you feel when you treat others that way when they
make mistakes?
How do others treat you when you make a mistake?
How do you feel when they treat you that way, give you grief?

We can either make a mess
of a mistake or bless a mistake.

The Curse of a Curse

Blowing out someone else's candle doesn't make yours shine any brighter.
—Unknown

If we give ourselves or others grief when a mistake is made, we are making the situation worse for everyone.

Jack Canfield, best-selling author of the *Chicken Soup for the Soul* series, told me a story. He made a mistake when he was driving, and the negative comments made to him kept him from getting his driver's license until four years after he was eligible.

To keep yourself from negatively impacting others, bless their mistakes. When someone impacts you in any negative way, bless the person for his or her mistake.

> *May you never be the reason why someone who loved to sing, doesn't anymore. Or why someone who dressed so uniquely, now wears plain clothing. Or why someone who always spoke so excitedly about their dreams, is now silent about them. May you never be the reason someone gave up on a part of themselves because you were demotivating, non-appreciative, hypercritical, or even worse—sarcastic about it.*
>
> —Mostafa Ibrahim

Support Is a Superpower

We rise by lifting others.
—Robert Ingersoll

When you do an act of kindness toward another person, you are supporting yourself. And as a result:

- You experience *instant gratification* because it's natural to support another person and unnatural to put someone down.
- You feel *instant inner well-being* because supportive kindness toward others is in you and naturally needs expression.
- Doing the act of kindness is an act of kindness toward yourself; you can feel it.

When we are in our natures, we naturally support ourselves and others.

- Think of someone who wants something that seems odd to you (an old Junker car, a book on spiders, unfamiliar clothing, bright colored hair, and so on). S/he (name of the person you're thinking about) likes or wants_____.
- Say and feel, "I don't like that."
- Feel the disapproval until it disappears.
- Feel what it feels like to have an opinion that differs from that person's.
  - Notice the tension.
- Feel what it feels like to support the person in what he or she wants.
- Say and feel, "They should do what they love to do. So should I."
  - Notice the freedom.

Giving support to another demonstrates sanity and humanity.

Acting Kindly Now and Now and Now

The smallest act of kindness is worth
more than the grandest intention.
—Oscar Wilde

Acting kindly is to be the recipient of well-being. In other words, when we act kindly, we feel kindly and receive that feeling.

Do it now and now and for the rest of today and for tomorrow, too. And when you forget to be kind, bless your mistake, and come back to kindness. That means notice the unkindness and correct yourself—make kindness your go-to.

Blessing mistakes is an act of kindness. Random acts of kindness have gained a lot of popularity because they bring out our True Natures and living from our True Natures *is* well-being.

Intentional Acts of Kindness

An act of kindness lifts you up, and you get to
share that lift with the world.

When you genuinely do something kind and want nothing in return, you will immediately feel more positive.

If it's a "pretend" or "egoic" act of kindness, it's painful, not quietly rewarding. If the act of kindness is cruel or mean it will show up then or later, causing you a lot of stress (the law of karma is activated, meaning action has happened—and all actions have consequences). An example would be pretending to be kind with a comment that is 'constructive criticism' that not's constructive, its intention is cruelty. One way to help with this is to ask yourself, if you can come back to your naturally kind nature and ask from there what a true act of kindness would be.

Kindness within Your Family
My dad's favorite toast was, "Here's to kindness." He learned a secret: When you are kind to others, they're kind to you. Or they're not, but you can stay in a state of kindness for your own well-being as much as you can.

One simple exercise to help stay in your naturally kind state within your family is to remind yourself how you feel when you are kind and remind yourself that *you* feel better when you're kind than when you're cruel to someone in your family.

A good resource for acts of kindness within your family is http:// naturalparentsnetwork.com/60-acts-of-kindness-for-our-families/.

Kindness in the Workplace
For your own well-being, be genuinely kind to people you work with when you can. You know what it feels like for someone to be kind to you at work. Pass it on!

A good resource for acts of kindness in the workplace is https://kyliehunt. com/random-acts-of-kindness/.

Acts of Kindness on the Road
Have you noticed that drivers bring their frustrations with them while they're driving their vehicles? For your own well-being, don't be one of them.

When others make driving mistakes, bless their mistakes, take slow, deep breaths, and stay present. Take care to ensure your own safety while they are jeopardizing everyone's. That means don't get drawn into the chaos. It's not a requirement!

Consider the alternatives:

- — Frustration
- — Impatience
- — Self-importance
- — Road rage danger

A good resource for acts of kindness on the road is https://www. randomactsofkindness.org/kindness-ideas/873-be-polite-on-the-road.

Kindness in Schools (excerpt from Edutopia.org)

> **Spread the Joy**
> Remind students that being kind doesn't require grand gestures. This free printable bookmark encourages students to make kindness a priority, and it works for all ages. Younger students can color it in, while older students can mark their place in their reading.
>
> A kindness flyer is another simple way to engage students in middle school in compassionate acts. Elementary students can use this free template to design a tear-off poster that can be displayed in classrooms or hallways. Older students can make a similar flyer by brainstorming a list of kind

actions and placing each on a tear-off portion of a flyer. Encourage students to take—and then actually do—the actions suggested by their classmates.
Grade levels: All

Gamify It
This bingo card from our archives can be printed and used to promote generous acts in the classroom. Students fill in each square when they take the specific action noted. The first person to fill the card wins.

Kindness Bingo
A kindness scavenger hunt, like this one from *Kiddie Matters*, can help elementary school students look for ways to be nice to one another. Students complete as many actions as

possible in a week. Teachers may choose to offer a prize for the student who completes the most, or allow the gift of generosity to be the only prize.
Grade levels: K–5

Encourage Small Acts of Kindness

At John C. Haines Elementary School in Chicago, students place a pom-pom in a jar when they do something nice for their peers and then describe the action to the class. Asking students to articulate their kindnesses and to work collaboratively to fill the jar reinforces a positive classroom culture. Once the jar is full, the entire class celebrates with a special treat or party.
Grade levels: pre-K–5

Go Digital

Leverage students' excitement for apps to encourage kindness. The free app Nobly aims to "build a culture of kindness" as a platform for users to record and share their good deeds. The app connects kind acts through hashtags called "chains," which allows students to see how their actions influence others to be kind.
Grade levels: 6–8; 9–12

Make It an Entire Month

One school in Cork, Ireland, Gaelscoil Mhichil Ui Choileain, replaces homework with acts of kindness for an entire month. Each day of the week has a theme: On Mondays, students communicate with an elderly person. On Tuesdays, they are tasked with helping their parents in some way. On Wednesdays, they find a random act of kindness to perform, and on Thursdays, they focus on self-care by doing something that makes them feel good about themselves. During the week students leave charitable observations of their peers in a "kindness bucket," and at a Friday assembly, the school shares a few of the kind thoughts. Throughout the month, students document and reflect on their actions in gratitude diaries.
Grade levels: 6–8; 9–12

Kindness toward Teachers
Imagine being a teacher!

I asked some teachers what the best acts of kindness they had received were, and they answered:

- Handwritten notes from parents, and especially from the kids (number 1 every time).
- Homemade food (after learning what the teacher likes).
- Gift cards (after learning where the teacher shops or eats out).
- Help in the classroom (after being approved as a volunteer).

Your Ideas for Acts of Kindness

1. Bless my mistakes.
2. Bless others' mistakes.
3. _____
4. _____
5. _____
6. _____
7. _____
8. _____
9. _____
10. _____

How to Respond to Rudeness, Meanness, and Bad Behavior

If it costs you peace,
It's too expensive.
—Unknown

People think, speak, and act from their beliefs. When they act out, it's because they have a false belief that they must uphold to achieve some sort of success, safety, and happiness.

For your own well-being, when others are acting out:

- Silently bless their mistakes to put yourself in the right frame of mind.
- Do your own inner work as soon as you see someone act out. Get quiet, see where you are that, feel it, and it will let go of you. We all have all behaviors; some are more latent than others. This simple strategy is see it, feel it, and be free of it.
- Remind yourself,
  - They can't do differently than they are; just like when we act out, we can't do differently until we can.
  - It's not our job to judge others (my dad's favorite saying to me).
  - It's not our job to teach everyone good manners.
  - It goes against our good natures to move out of our natures.
  - Their behaviors are about them; don't make it about you by engaging in the same way.

As Eckhart Tolle, an awakened spiritual teacher, points out, if you don't like a situation, change it, leave it, or accept it. All else is madness.

Being Hard on Myself

"Blessing Mistakes has been such a valuable tool for me to have, both for my own use and for using with others. It helped me to gain the awareness of how hard I'd been on myself throughout my life when it came to mistakes. Being hard on myself for mistakes made had never actually helped me though.

Using this technique, I'm put in the right frame of mind to actually help myself learn from the mistake and come up with productive solutions.

It absolutely helps me parent better. I can help my kids effectively use their mistakes to learn and grow and let them go. It helps "take the heat" out of those times when someone does something that turns out to be the tipping point into big emotional upsets. Life doesn't have to be as intense as we make it. This technique helps with that!

It also has helped me to forgive and heal when dealing with wrongdoings of others.

Blessing Mistakes is a game-changer for me. Talk. About. Relief.

Using this technique with others really helps put a person in a space of empathy. This definitely helps you to change your mindset and interact with the person differently, which also opens the space to finding solutions vs. victim blame.

Sometimes people have the misperception that this approach doesn't allow for accountability. But because this approach changes the victim-blame narrative, it actually allows for greater opportunity for exploring behaviours.

Plus, it can be fun, and you can end up laughing over some mistakes instead of having them ruin your mood or day!"

Janna Glasman, CBP, BAT, PCP,
Mom, Franklin Method Educator,
Meditation Coach, Kid Code Teacher

Buried Alive

If we bury a mistake, it stays alive inside of us, causing unease.
If we bless it, the stress around it dissolves.

If we defend a mistake, it stays alive inside us to make us offensive.
If we bless it, we experience Grace.

If we deny a mistake, it stays alive inside us to make us dishonest.
If we bless it, it humbles us.

If we make an excuse for a mistake, it stays alive inside us to disempower us.
If we bless it, we feel peaceful and powerful.

Doing anything other than taking responsibility for a mistake when we make one, and blessing ourselves for it, causes us much stress.

Doing anything other than blessing someone else for a mistake causes the person and us much stress.

Well-Being: The Mystery

(It's the same as being in our True Natures.)

It's not hard to find
When you look in the right places.

Well-being is being happy and grateful on the inside, no matter what's happening on the outside.

Where Well-Being Is
Well-being is installed as our natural operating systems (like we see in kids). Currently, it's largely obscured by identification. Identification is attachment to an idea/opinion/thought that we learned and adopted in childhood that's not true that we thought would make us safe, happy, healthy, and successful.

We see reflections of our True Natures—which is well-being—when we look at the sky and feel expansive, or look at a mountain and feel the stillness, or look at a young child and feel innocence. Those states are our True Natures noticed by us in different situations.

Where Well-Being Isn't
Another person can't give well-being to us. It can't be found by simply getting something we want or by doing anything. And we can't find well-being in an organization, event, or a situation. However, we *can* bring well-being into everything we do because it is our innate way of being.

Looking outside us for what's inside us is like getting clues
to where the treasure's hidden and then
running in the opposite direction.

My Experience with Blessing Mistakes

Creating Connection

"Grama, you're supposed to pick me up at six o'clock, after dance class."

"I usually pick you up at seven o'clock. Did something change?"

"No, but I know it's six o'clock."

I arrived at six o'clock, feeling a bit puzzled. But she was old enough to know, and I thought something must have changed since I last picked her up from dance.

When I got to the studio, she didn't come out like she usually did. So I went in, and she said, with a sheepish look on her face, that I was supposed to pick her up at seven o'clock.

I went home and stewed over it a bit, until I realized I needed to use blessing mistakes on the situation. I blessed myself for stewing over the mistake: "I matter more than the mistake of stewing about it." I felt the relief and the return to my True Nature, so when she got in the car after class, apologized, and then waited in trepidation to see if she was in trouble, I was able to say (and feel the truth of it), "Bless you, honey. You matter more than the mistake."

I hadn't shared this strategy with my kids or grandkids yet, so she didn't know what to make of it. But she knew the feeling of not being in trouble for a mistake. She didn't say anything for a few seconds, and then quietly said, "Thank you, Grama."

I just thank my lucky stars that this work has come to me and that I can use it to create connection and respect instead of rejection, disconnection, and discord.

From a Curse (the Nasty Kind) to a Blessing

One day I drove over the curb while I was leaving a drive-through. My husband was with me, and he got to witness the event as it unfolded.

As soon as I drove over it, I had a flash of upset and the thought that if I kept doing that, I would need new tires, and I was wasting and disrespecting the earth by not being careful how I used its resources. That took a second or two. At the same time, I said a very unpolite word. Then I came to my senses, blessed myself, and said aloud, "I matter more than the mistake." The stress disappeared. My husband and I laughed, serious uproarious laughter for several minutes. It was such an amazing experience to go from upset and cursing to joy in the span of a couple of seconds by using this simple pointer back to my True Nature.

Relationship Building

There is a remarkable softness that comes over me when my husband blesses me for a mistake.

There is a remarkable softness that comes over me when I bless myself or another for a mistake.

Life is too short to be upset, even for a minute.

When my dad said, "It doesn't matter a particle," when I put that dent in his truck, and he opened his two big arms wide to me so I could walk into them for a hug, I experienced joy and gratitude in every single cell of my body. I know a blessing when I feel one, and that one was so big that it became a way of living peacefully.

When I say to someone, "You matter more than the mistake," I don't feel any of the awful feelings that accompany judging a mistake. When I bless another for his or her mistake, I'm blessing myself with well-being.

When we give Grace,

We get Grace.

You won't know that

Until you feel it.

Hurry—bless a mistake!

CHAPTER 2

Blessing Mistakes

(Excerpt from The Kid Code, 30 Second Parenting Strategies)

All people who make mistakes,
big or small, deserve love.
Karma takes care of their consequences.
Your kindness takes care of yours.

Learning how to give yourself and others Grace, not grief, when a mistake is made is for everyone's well-being. With a clear understanding of it, it can reduce the stress in a household by 50 percent on the first day of using it!

This stress-reducing, connection-creating strategy will change how you feel inside of yourself, how you feel toward others, and how others feel toward you. It puts the focus on the human being, not the mistake, and it points us back to our True Nature.

Use this with your kids, partners, friends, family, coworkers; use it with anyone and everyone—even with yourself.

It's natural to support someone when a mistake is made. How we know this to be true, is to see how we feel inside of ourselves when we offer true support and want nothing in return.

Whatever feels natural *is* natural.

It doesn't feel natural to belittle, humiliate, embarrass, disgrace, shame, or dishonor someone when they make a mistake. How we know this to be true is that if we check inside ourselves while behaving in those ways, we don't feel good or natural.

The first thing to do the instant a mistake is made, as taught by Janna Glasman, a Kid Code teacher, is to give yourself an innocent 'reminder word or phrase'—like "oops" or "no need for chaos"—that will spark the idea of using blessing mistakes. This helps shift the brain away from the old, negatively programmed reaction to this new humane way of addressing mistakes with a blessing.

1. **Someone else makes a mistake.**

The mistake is already done, so now you can decide how you want to be and feel and act toward the person who made the mistake. Do you want to give them grief (be mean) or give them Grace (be kind)?

> If you give them grief, notice how awful you feel while you do it and how awful you feel long after you've done it (the misery keeps coming back when we talk to ourselves in our heads, either justifying our position or berating the other person).

> If you give them Grace, notice how good you feel while you do it (it's a compassionate, non-judgmental feeling). Giving the other Grace means showing kindness toward them.

It doesn't hurt to remember that we all still make many mistakes every day. That will help us want to give others Grace.

You say to them and feel the truth of the statement: "You matter more than the mistake." Use whatever language you feel conveys that the mistake doesn't devalue the person making it. Examples of what to say are:

"Everyone makes mistakes."

"Mistakes are often helpful!"

"Mistakes are not meant to make us feel bad."

"When I make a mistake, I bless myself because it's kind to do that."

"This mistake doesn't matter—you do."

"Making mistakes doesn't make a person bad."

"Making mistakes is inevitable."

"I feel good when I bless my mistake and then make it right."

"Some mistakes are meant to be a lesson to help us along the way."

"Sometimes I get it wrong many times before I get it right."

2. **Part 2 of blessing mistakes: Make it right, learn from it, let it go.**

Make It Right

That means apologize, replace something, clean up something, or whatever will make it right. Why?

Making it right feels good inside.

Each of us is 100 percent responsible for whatever we say or do. We think everyone else is responsible for what they say and do, so by that logic, we are also responsible for everything we say and do. Denial of a mistake or justifying a mistake feels bad inside of us. We don't want to make ourselves feel bad; we're aiming for our own well-being, not misery.

Learn from It

See if there is a lesson that can help you. "What did I learn that I'd like to change?"

Maybe there is nothing to learn.

Let It Go

Once you've made the mistake right and/or learned from it, there is nothing else to do but to let it go. Leave it in the past, where is it. Holding on hurts.

Let it go means:

- Feel the uncomfortable feelings that arise around the mistake until they disappear. By facing and feeling the feelings that arise every time they arise, we are aiding in dissolving them. We can't dissolve the truth, but since it's not true that we're meant to feel bad, any negative feeling can be dissolved.
- Invite yourself to "burn it up," as taught by Guy Finley, a self-realized spiritual teacher. That means think about the mistake and ask for it to be burned up, burned out of your consciousness. Feel what you feel until there is a release.
- Offer it to the Universe to transform it.
- Surrender to making a mistake, and let it naturally dissolve. Surrendering the mistake means we give up fighting and resisting that we made a mistake or that we feel bad about it.
- Some other strategies for letting go are to imagine putting the mistake on the wind and let it blow away or put it in a box that contains all mistakes and neutralizes them just outside of your house.

3. **You make a mistake.**

> *Place your mistakes under your feet*
> *and use them as stepping-stones.*
> —Unknown

Bless yourself by saying to yourself and feeling the truth of the statement, "I matter so much more than this mistake."

Make the mistake right as best as you can. Learn from it, and then let it go and leave it in the past.

4. **Someone makes a mistake, and you give them grief.**

Bless yourself for making the mistake of giving them grief, and make it right with them. This is for your own well-being, and theirs.

5. **You are negative.**

Being negative is not part of your nature, so it's a mistake. As soon as you notice you are thinking, feeling, speaking, or acting in a negative way, stop yourself, and say and feel the truth of the statement, "I matter so much more than this mistake of being negative."

6. **The other person is negative.**

As soon as you notice another person has a negative expression on his or her face, or is speaking or acting in a negative way, *silently* say to yourself, and feel the truth of the statement said towards that person, "You matter so much more than the mistake of being negative." This is designed to give you relief by pointing you back to the truth and to your nature. It's not about the other person. They may not think they've made a mistake and that's not our business. Our business is our well-being.

The "Mistake Footprint"

When we don't bless a mistake, we leave a "mistake footprint" inside ourselves. That means we leave discomfort inside ourselves, and it will arise another day in another painful way. Anything that's not true inside of causes discomfort and repeatedly rises up to be seen and dissolved.

It's healthier to resolve a mistake in the moment it's made.

Please teach anyone who is interested to reduce stress levels around mistakes. Be part of the movement!

Being Negative Is a Mistake

You didn't form your ego.
You observed.
Then it formed you.
Now it's your (negative) operating system.

That little pearl of wisdom is paraphrased from Guy Finley. It means that when we were little our senses gathered, and stored, events attached to thoughts and feelings that became memory which became our operating system.

Memory is meant for practical applications, not to store hurts and bring then up as a way to deal with what's happening 10, 20, 30, 40, 50 or even 60 years later. This is a remarkably freeing understanding. We didn't form our personalities. Our memories stored negative events and emotions and we're still operating on those—until we arrive back at our essential nature.

Negativity is not normal. It's negative.

Negativity is not natural. It's unnatural. All we have to do to prove that to ourselves is to notice how we feel when we're negative.

Negativity comes from an identified part of ourselves, a conditioned, learned idea of who we are. It comes from one's ego.

An ego-identified personality thinks it's gaining something by being negative. Therefore, it keeps negativity at the ready as a strategy—a poor one—for life.

Here are some examples of what we believe we gain by being negative:

- I am right.
- I am the authority.

- I am smarter than another person.
- I am better than another person.
- I will get what I want.

The ego is the opposite of our essential natures, which are never negative. That's why it's a mistake when we're ego-identified and then become ego-operated.

When we're negative, we can reset ourselves by blessing the mistake. It's a way to self-regulate and lift ourselves out of negativity.

When another person is negative, we can bless the mistake instead of becoming entangled in the negativity and making the situation worse.

How Not to Use Blessing Mistakes

Deciding what not to do is as important
as deciding what to do.
—Charles Spurgeon

Don't Use Them to Avoid Responsibility
If you make a mistake and bless yourself but don't make the mistake right, you are not giving yourself the relief that blessing mistakes can give you. It can't be used to avoid responsibility. As a reminder, if someone else makes a mistake, who is responsible? They are of course. Remember that simple logic, when *we* make a mistake, *we* are responsible. Bless yourself for not taking responsibility, and then take responsibility.

Notice how you feel inside when you take responsibility rather than make excuses, justify, or deny making a mistake.

Don't Use It Out Loud When the Other Doesn't Think He or She Made a Mistake
You can't say, "Bless you," out loud to someone who doesn't think he or she has made a mistake. It will just make the individual angry and more defensive. You can silently say and feel, "Bless you," to them. That's for your own well-being and to help you not get entangled in a negative situation.

Don't Use It Out Loud with Strangers
Don't bless the actions of strangers unless you have a strong feeling that it's the right thing to do. They may not think they made a mistake and won't receive it well. They may think you are overstepping your bounds. And you are if ego is involved.

Mom, That Felt So Nice

"Blessing mistakes is a true blessing for me, for how I parent, and for my family.

It really changed my approach to parenting, and it also created an atmosphere of gentleness within our family dynamic.

I remember the first time I used this with my daughter. She had just finished spilling something all over the table and floor, and my response was, "Bless you. Let's clean it up." For a few seconds, it was like time stood still, and then she looked at me and said, "Mom that felt so nice." In that moment we got to experience the pleasure of our True Natures in a state of beingness.

As we continued using this tool for well-being, we all naturally began to say, "Bless you" more often. We found ourselves working as a team to fix the mistakes. The focus wasn't on the mistake; it was on valuing each other and on doing what needed to be done to make the mistake right.

Blessing mistakes is not only used by me. It has rippled outward and allowed the kids to start using it to bless each other and me."

Lasha Watson
Kid Code Instructor

Examples of When to Bless
Others for Their Mistakes

Escalate or ease—you choose.

– They spilled the milk.
  Spilled milk doesn't matter as much as the person does.
– They told a lie.
  While we want to teach our kids that lying causes their stress level to rise (proven by a lie detector test). Every time we lie, we set off internal stress. Invite kids to notice this after you've noticed it yourself. The lie doesn't matter as much as the person does.
– They stole your pocket change.
  Part 2 of blessing mistakes is making it right. If they stole your pocket change, hold them to paying it back. But the person still matters more than the mistake.
– Your partner missed a turn on the highway, and now you're going to be late.
  The person matters more than the mistake. There is no good in devaluing or even blaming him or her. Prove that to yourself.
– They made a mistake in investing your money.
  Being mad won't get the money back. Can you live without that money? Can you live with devaluing another human being? If you imagine what it feels like to devalue another person, you'll know you don't want to live that way.
– They put a dent in the car.
  "It doesn't matter a particle."
– They are negative.
  The person is more important than their behavior.

The person matters more than the mistake—always—
no matter how big the mistake is.

The goal here is to bring us back to our natures and not be drawn into our lower nature (the nature that lives in negativity and is not natural). It's not to vindicate anyone of wrongdoing. Karma will have to take care of that because we can't.

Think of one person you know who has made a big mistake.

- Remembering that they couldn't do any differently than they did because they didn't know any different, silently say and feel the truth of the statement, "You matter more than the mistake."
- Feel all the feelings that arise and repeat if you don't feel a shift into neutrality or compassion.
- If you don't shift into compassion right away, ask what other feelings you need to feel fully so you can free yourself. Things like resentment, fear or anger might come up. Feel them fully until they dissolve and then repeat the statement, "You matter more than the mistake," while feeling the truth of it because a human being is more important than their behaviors. Said another way, if we were to measure life against behaviors, which is more important?

Now make a list of mistakes the people in your life have made that still bother you and bless them for it. This will help you put blessing mistakes into action in real time.

Please repeat the above process as many times as it takes for you to soften. Remembering that our own acceptance and softening doesn't condone wrongdoings, it just lets us relax into a state we want to live from.

When I did this to relieve myself of my upset aimed at a bully, it took me seven times of doing this exercise before I began to feel free. I wanted to hang onto the hatred (for no good reason) until it dissolved and then I wondered why I would ever want to hang on to it.

Examples of When to Bless Yourself When You Make a Mistake

You make mistakes, mistakes don't make you.
—Maxwell Maltz

1. You burn supper.
    *   Say and feel the truth of the statement, "I matter more than my mistake." Being upset won't change what has already happened.
2. You interrupt someone.
    *   Say and feel the truth of the statement, "I matter more than this mistake."
3. You hollered at a partner/friend/stranger.
    *   Say and feel the truth of the statement, "I matter more than the mistake of losing my temper. It's not right, and I'm going to work on it. But in this moment, it's true that I matter more than the mistake." Remind yourself of this. Then make it right. Apologize.
4. You make any parenting mistake (you'll know it's a mistake because you won't feel good inside of yourself. Some examples are punishing, criticizing or shaming a child).
    *   Say and feel the truth of the statement, "I matter more than the parenting mistake I made. By blessing mistakes, I am becoming a more conscious parent. I am a work in progress, like all parents are." Make the mistake right.
5. You feel full of regret for your actions or words against another human being, be it today, yesterday, or fifty years ago.
    *   Say and feel the truth of the statement, "I matter more than the mistakes I made. I couldn't have done any differently because I didn't know any differently then." Now focus on how to make the mistakes right. If you hurt a child, help that child, even if he or she is grown. Find ways to help kids in general. If you hurt a friend and that friend has passed,

find something good to do to honor that friend. This switch from problem-oriented thinking to forgiveness and then proactive goodness will bring you back into your nature, a place you are meant to live from.

6. You have negative thoughts, speak negatively to another person, or act negatively. After you bless yourself for the mistake, you can make it right. Say, and feel the truth of the statement:
    *   "I matter more than the mistake of negative thinking."
    *   "I matter more than the mistake I made of speaking in a negative way."
    *   "I matter more than the mistake of acting negatively."
7. You judge or criticize—beat up on—yourself.
    *   Say and feel the truth of the statement, "I matter more than this mistake of beating up on myself."
8. You rant and rave at yourself or another.
    *   Say and feel the truth of the statement, "I matter more than this mistake of ranting and raving."
    *   Bless yourself.

There is no good reason to be upset with yourself.
There is always good reasons to bless yourself
and make your mistake right.
You will never regret being kind to yourself.

Blessing Mistakes Is Really Quite Magical!

"Saying and feeling, "You matter more than the mistake," takes me out of fear, judgement, and stress back to a calm, compassionate me.

Just the thought of blessing mistakes can take me out of attack mode. And it happens in a second, just as quickly as it takes to blink, instant relief! I still need an external prompt to remember to do it, but I'm getting better!

Anytime, anywhere, instant relief to diffuse any stressful situation.

And it's fun to watch the relief take over when I remind myself or a friend of the opportunity to bless a mistake! All the tension melts away!"

Lesia Dubik
Competency Development Specialist
Government of Manitoba

The Bliss Barometer

Make space in your life
for what matters.
—Unknown

Except for when we're sleeping in bed, we are always in one of two states:

- Ego-operated
- Nature-operated (Natural, Isness, True Nature, Essential Nature, Source, The Field, Zero Point)

When we are ego-operated, there is a noticeable feeling of wanting something, or a feeling of unease that makes us seek fulfillment. We also experience some level of discomfort or upset.

When we are nature-operated, we are at ease. There are levels to this state. It can be neutral, meaning no charge; this doesn't mean one is apathetic. In any natural state where there is a feeling of nothing wrong, all is right. One will experience:

- Feeling gratitude for no reason
- Feeling relaxed
- Feeling genuine
- Feeling compassionate
- Feeling joyful
- Feeling creative
- Feeling playful
- Feeling inclusive

The highest state is blissful aliveness.

You have a built-in "bliss barometer." As soon as you move out of the state of nature-operated into ego-operated, you can bless yourself for your mistake. That will move you back into being in your nature.

When we're in ego-operated states, the bliss barometer is on the low end of the scale. When we're nature-operated, it is on the high end of the scale.

Check your bliss barometer regularly and move yourself back into well-being!

I want to be a decent, loving human being.

I am not happy when I'm not.

I don't feel good inside myself when I'm not.

I don't know why I can't do that.

I will use blessing mistakes all day,

every day (say it and feel it) with myself and with others

to point me to what I am:

a decent loving human being.

Because that's who I am when I'm in my nature.

Am I obliged to be a decent, loving human being? Yes.

What will take me there?

Loving the Lesson

Forget the mistake, remember the lesson.
—Roald Dahl

There are no mistakes in life, only lessons.
—Robin Sharma

...You can't learn anything being perfect.
—Adam Osborne

*I've learned so much from my mistakes, I'm
thinking of making a few more.*
—Cheryl Cole

*Every mistake adds marginally
to your wisdom bank.*
—M. K. Soni

*Mistakes have the power to turn you into
something better than you were before.*
—Unknown

*Experience is simply the name
we give our mistakes.*
—Oscar Wilde

Once a mistake has been made and made right, go deeper.

Is there something to learn, or can I leave this in the past, where it is?

Sitting quietly can help uncover lessons. Giving our attention in this way and asking, "What can I learn?" is an invitation for the answer to appear. As Eckhart Tolle teaches, get quiet, ask the question, stay for a minute or two in Stillness, and then come out of that state into focused thinking. When we go into Stillness—get still in body and mind—answers come because the Universe focuses on solutions, not problems. This is real self-help all the way back to our nature which always knows what to do and say because it's basic operating mechanism is peace and harmlessness. Our nature doesn't need help. It is help.

Turn your state of mind from attitude to gratitude.
Go from attitude for a lesson or a mistake to gratitude for a lesson or a mistake. Say and feel the truth of the words, "Thank you for the lesson. Otherwise, I wouldn't have known I was living outside of my nature." Going from grumpy to grateful isn't a big leap; it's a decision.

> *All the ups and downs are Grace*
> *in different wrappings,*
> *sent to refine consciousness.*
> *Say thanks to them all.*
> —Mooji, spiritual teacher

Some of our mistakes are excellent.
What mistakes have you made that are?

Attention Determines Our Destinies

Pay attention to what you're paying attention to.
—Unknown

This section is to help us avoid serious *mistakes, if possible*, like car accidents, falling down stairs, and accidents that have painful and potentially life altering consequences.

Where was my attention when I made the mistake?

As Guy Finley points out, "Where goes my attention, so comes my experience." Many mistakes can be avoided by keeping our attention in the here and now. If our attention is actually on what we're doing, and not wandering into the past or the future, we're less likely to make a mistake in the first place. For example, if my attention isn't on the stairs I'm walking up, I'm more likely to trip. My mind is useful for attending to every step while walking up or down them. If I'm in the "there and then"—thinking about the past or future—and not the here and now, my mind will not be useful for what's happening in the moment. If I'm thinking about a past or future event, I can't be here now where I am to protect and care for myself and others. If my attention isn't on the hammer, kitchen knife, vacuum, road, and so on, I'm more likely to make a mistake. These mistakes may be small or large. They may even be deadly.

Until we can keep our attention where we are, bless every mistake for our own well-being.

And to help us stay more present with our attention on what's happening in the moment, ponder this:

Watch your thoughts;
They become words
Watch your words;

47

They become actions
Watch your actions;
They become habits
Watch your habits;
They become character;
It becomes your destiny.
—Lao Tzu

Bless your negative thoughts, words, actions, habits, and character to change your destiny.

Arrogance, I Don't Need You Anymore

A mistake that makes you humble is better than
an achievement that makes you arrogant.
—Unknown

Apologizing to another person is for your well-being, and it makes the mistake right. It puts us right with the world and with other human beings. Apologizing hurts one's self-image—terribly—while we do it. Before you apologize, remind yourself, "This is gonna' hurt my 'I'm right,' self. But I want to be right with the world, so I'm going to do it." It won't kill you—it will just feel like it, temporarily.

The more you do this, the freer you become.

Live like this: I need no apology. This is true because my essential nature doesn't need an apology to be okay. And I need to apologize to everyone I've hurt. This is true because apologizing makes me a decent human being, and that's what I truly want to be. If you really need an apology, as spiritual teacher Byron Katie says, give yourself one.

Practice apologizing—but only in a genuine way—every chance you get:

1. "I'm sorry for …"
2. My favorite to my husband: "Would you please excuse me for a minute. I need to go kick the pedestal out from underneath myself." Then I go and sit quietly and see what this identity is, feel what it's doing to me and others, and then go back and apologize. I want to be a decent human being because not being decent is painful.

You don't want to hurt.
Not apologizing hurts.

Acceptance Is Forgiveness

The weak can never forgive.
Forgiveness is the attribute of the strong.
—Mahatma Gandhi

Forgiving another person is for your well-being. Byron Katie tells us, "Forgiveness is just another name for freedom." Our freedom.

We suffer when we don't forgive another person. Forgiving another person doesn't mean you agree with what he or she did or said. It means you're taking care of your well-being.

Jack Canfield says that when people hurt us, it isn't personal. They would do what they did to anyone.

If you have been hurt by another's mistaken words and actions toward you, get on your knees. This position helps your innate humbleness appear, which is an indication of your inner strength. Then say silently to them, "I know you couldn't do any different than you did because you believed what you believed. I forgive you."

While you're down there, it's helpful to say, "I accept that I can't forgive easily. I've been mistaken in my understanding. I know that forgiveness of another is for me too."

Don't get up yet! Guy Finley points out that if we haven't forgiven, we need to look at the reality: We have found a reason to hate. "I'm sorry I have hatred in me."

You'll never know how strong your heart is
until you learn to forgive who broke it.
—Byron Katie

Ubuntu

Be kind whenever possible.
It's always possible.
—His Holiness The 14th Dalai Lama

The idea of supporting another person when he or she makes a mistake is not new.

Ubuntu is an African social philosophy/culture in which the community comes together for the common good. The application of this strategy is similar to restorative justice, where all parties involved are treated respectfully but are still responsible for their actions.

This tradition, when it's practically applied, uncovers our peaceful, inclusive nature. It uncovers what feels best to us inside us, leaving everyone involved with their dignity intact, creating harmony between all parties involved, finding justice, and demonstrating caring and compassion.

When someone does something wrong, the members of the community put him or her in the center of a circle and then spend two days talking about all the good that individual has done. The basis for this kind of intervention is the belief that people are inherently good, and this will encourage them to reconnect with that part of themselves. This positive approach points to what other cultures also know to be true: changing behavior is more effective with unified affirmation of another's goodness than by using shame and punishment.

Ubuntu is a cure for perpetrator and victim behaviors because it dissolves the insecurity that causes those states in a human being.

Ubuntu is also (much longer) version of blessing mistakes. You can take a minute to genuinely say something that's truly good about another person and make a difference—we don't need to take two days, although the more time you spend doing this, the more you help the other person rehabilitate and self-regulate back to their nature—as long as you are genuine.

ubuntu

In certain regions of South Africa, when someone does something wrong, he is taken to the center of the village and surrounded by his tribe for two days while they speak of all the good he has done. They believe each person is good, yet sometimes we make mistakes, which is really a cry for help. They unite in this ritual to encourage the person to reconnect with his true nature. The belief is that unity and affirmation have more power to change behavior than shame and punishment. This is known as Ubuntu - humanity towards others.

Restorative Justice

No one has ever become poor
by giving.
—Anne Frank

Restorative justice is a practical system born out of a social philosophy that puts the priority as relationship-based solutions for social violations.

It brings together those involved in wrongdoing to get everyone involved in what they need to make it right.

Blessing mistakes contributes to this humanitarian way of dealing with violations. It instantly relieves the stress around wrongdoing for everyone involved.

In my experience, all wrongdoings are mistakes because if we were in our natural selves, operating from what feels natural inside us, we would never have the impulse to do wrong.

To me, restorative justice, Ubuntu, and blessing mistakes offer positive solutions to any wrongdoing because they both work to bring out the natural goodness in a human being *while* ensuring justice is restored.

When we unknowingly adopt the role of the victim or the perpetrator, we *will* suffer those roles. If we bring understanding to why we, as part of a peace movement want to dissolve the victim and the perpetrator within ourselves by blessing our mistake of adopting those roles, we free ourselves of these painful ways of experiencing life.

The Victim

If a victim can honestly address the offender and say and feel the truth of this statement, "You matter more than the mistake," they would begin to free themselves of victimhood. The importance is placed on the person, rather than on the mistake or violation.

Victims don't want to feel like victims. There is no valid gain in doing so. Victims become helpless, powerless, incapacitated, resentful, and bitter. They want retribution, which births violence that they direct toward themselves and/or others. As Byron Katie says, victims are the most violent people on the planet. That's easier to see in war-torn countries, where the perpetrator makes a victim out of someone, and the victim retaliates. There is no solution in this no-exit loop of back-and-forth retribution and resentment. These ways of living don't solve problems; they make more of them.

It is true that when we become victims we want to lash out as one way to make things right. The victims' form of justice is often to punish others and/or themselves. As we'll discuss later in the book, the whole paradigm of punishment doesn't deliver what it promises. It doesn't change bad behavior into good behavior.

It's more difficult to see in ourselves. But let's look so we can set ourselves free of victimhood if it does exist inside of us.

Think of a time when you were a victim: when someone repeatedly insulted you or picked on you, gaslighted you, continuously falsely accused you, when they stole something from you or swerved in front of you to cut you off in traffic and you had to slam on the brakes, putting yourself and others at risk. This sets us up to label them as the perpetrator and us as the victim. We can get mildly upset all the way to outraged—we want to lash out at them. In any case, we're poisoning ourselves with our negativity and with the adoption of a role or identity of a victim that isn't natural to us.

The offender isn't right, but that's not a good reason for us to take on and live from the helpless, violent victim identity. You can feel the discomfort of a victim identity inside yourself. We don't need it anymore.

What's true is that the victim doesn't want to feel like a victim.

When you notice you are feeling like a victim, you're unable to operate out of your True Nature. It's helpful to re-route your thinking, say, and feel the truth of the statement, "I matter more than the mistake of believing I need to stay a victim."

The Offender (Perpetrator)
All offenders are taught to be offenders. They are not bad people; they are people with bad behaviors. They don't really want to be offenders. They just don't know anything different. An offender experiences remorse, anger, disconnection, despair, and rejection. No one wants to feel those things.

At the same time, they are, as we are, one hundred percent responsible for their behaviors.

How we know this to be true is to check inside ourselves and see how we feel, use our own bliss barometers. When we are acting out of a natural place, our bliss barometers give us a natural high! When we are acting out of an unnatural place (violating someone else), our bliss barometers give us an unnatural low. All negative states register negatively on the barometer because we're out of alignment with our True Natures.

If there is a 'high' while acting out, it's always false. It's a fix or a feed for the attachment or identity that is commanding the action.

Restorative justice includes a broader field known as restorative practice. It addresses repairing the harm done and finding a positive way forward.

Blessing mistakes is a restorative practice because it teaches people another way to bring themselves into their joyful, harmless natures. Actions from that place are always positive and solution-oriented, so taking responsibility for any wrongdoing is actually a relief.

When we lash out at anyone, we are an offender. It's easy to see that role doesn't serve us well.

When you notice you've identified as an offender, say to yourself, and feel the truth of the statement, "I matter so much more than the mistake of attaching to this role of being an offender as though it's my right and purpose."

Do these systems really work?

Restorative Justice: Where's the Evidence?
The following is an excerpt from the Smith Institute showing restorative justice is effective.

A review of research on restorative justice (RJ) in the UK and abroad shows that across 36 direct comparisons to conventional criminal justice (CJ), RJ has, in at least two tests each:

- substantially reduced repeat offending for some offenders, but not all;
- doubled (or more) the offences brought to justice as diversion from CJ;
- reduced crime victims' post-traumatic stress symptoms and related costs;
- provided both victims and offenders with more satisfaction with justice than CJ;
- reduced crime victims' desire for violent revenge against their offenders;
- reduced the costs of criminal justice, when used as diversion from CJ;
- reduced recidivism (reoffending) *more than* prison (adults) or *as well as* prison (youths).

Restorative Justice: The Evidence. 2007. P. 4. Date accessed: May 09, 2021. (http://www.smith-institute.org.uk/wp-content/uploads/2015/10/RestorativeJusticeTheEvidenceFullreport.pdf)

"There is support that restorative justice is evidence-based for school discipline."

WestEd Justice & Prevention Research Center, a nonprofit research and service agency, conducts research into school safety, violence, and crime prevention, says that restorative justice in schools led to increased connectedness and decreased fighting, suspensions, and bullying. *Restorative Justice in U.S. Schools*. March 2019. Date accessed: May 10, 2021. (https://www.wested.org/wp-content/uploads/2019/04/resource-restorative-justice-in-u-s-schools-an-updated-research-review.pdf).

Improves Victim/Offender Satisfaction
The government of Canada compared nonrestorative approaches and restorative justice and found, "restorative justice to be more successful at achieving each of its four major goals." That means that everyone is better served with a more compassionate approach to solving problems. *The Effectiveness of Restorative Justice Practices: A Meta-Analysis. January 18, 2018. P. 1. Date accessed: May 11, 2021.* (https://www.justice.gc.ca/eng/rp-pr/csj-sjc/jsp-sjp/rp01_1-dr01_1/p5.html).

Restorative Justice to Help with Bullying and Suicide
A 2012 report from the US Attorney General's office states, "Restorative practices are especially helpful for children and youth who engage in and are harmed by bullying." They further state that it is, "an essential step in stopping the spread of emotional and physical violence toward children."

The report goes on to say that restorative practices have evidence-based success in suicide prevention programs. *Report of the Attorney General's National Task Force On Children Exposed to Violence*. December 12, 2012. P. 154. Date accessed May 12, 2021. (http://www.justice.gov/defendingchildhood/cev-rpt-full.pdf)

Your own evidence of wanting a peaceful resolution
for everyone is inside you.

Bullying Is the Opposite of Blessing

Strike me down and I'll
become more powerful
than you can imagine.
—Unknown

It's a big problem—with an interesting solution.

People who bully have not been blessed by others. That doesn't excuse their behaviors. They are still responsible for what they say and do.

If you have a bully in your house, start blessing his or her mistakes. It will help the bully feel more secure, and that security will help him or her lose interest in bullying.

While that's a good start, it would be helpful to complete the course on bullying, *BullyProof Yourself & Your Kids,* at www.thekidcode.ca. This course will help you and your kids become educated about bullies, meet and defeat the bully and learn about bully basics, bully buttons, bully tactics and BullyProof Strategies.

What Comes Naturally to Us Works

Look deep into nature and you will understand everything better.
—Albert Einstein

If it comes naturally in nature—it *works*.

It's natural for the leaves to fall from the tree and become fertilizer for the tree, helping to make new leaves in the spring. What's natural works.

Giving another person a blessing when a mistake is made works because it's natural.

If thoughts, words, actions, and behaviors feel natural, they work. If they don't feel natural, they're not natural, and they don't work. That means any negativity, because it doesn't feel natural, isn't natural. A negative state doesn't work, serve, or accomplish what we hoped it would by using it.

Cascading Cooperation

When I do good, I feel good.
When I do bad, I feel bad.
That's my religion.
—Abraham Lincoln

A research article from Princeton University demonstrates that when you do good, it does more good than the good you did—because when you're kind, there is a ripple effect. In fact, goodness triples itself!

Cooperative behavior cascades in human social networks. James H. Fowler and Nicholas A. Christakis. March 8, 2012. P. 1. Date accessed: May 08, 2021 (https://www.pnas.org/content/early/2010/02/25/0913149107.abstract?sid=269b1a48-0549-4109-998c-da1be87ed3c7)

Does anyone really need a study to understand this to be true?

A mistake doesn't take us out of well-being, how we react does.

Bless mistakes, and let it ripple!

Two Simple Words That Have Profound Impact

> "Bless you (me!)" Two very simple words that I had no idea would impact my life in the profound way they have. I began using them, simply, when I spilt something, or when someone around me did. The lack of tension I felt as a result, and the smile and "thank you, Mom," it brought naturally made me want to use, "Bless you," more.

> Blessing mistakes has become my go-to and part of my everyday moments. It is a pointer that anytime I feel tension inside, I bless myself and, if needed, the other. Blessing my mistake allows me to take a breath, which creates even the

tiniest of space to catch myself that something within me is off. Blessing mistakes tells me when I am not present.

Blessing mistakes helps me explore deeper what is a "mistake," and what causes "mistakes" to happen. I am learning that when we are gripped in identity, we are no different than a tiny, innocent child who does not know better. As tiny, innocent children, we need our mistakes blessed, not harshly reprimanded.

From this space of blessing, I can then see with more clarity what needs to be done to correct my mistake, and that, too, happens naturally.

I am seeing the countless ways I can use blessing mistakes. I am understanding that any negative state is a result of a false identity and, therefore, a mistake. To bless the other's identity and bless my own, instead of reacting in that identified state, allows something within me to pause and untangle, creating space and clarity.

I want to live consciously. I want to laugh, play, and accept as children do. Blessing mistakes is my segue into a more conscious, joyful, and loving way to live! Blessing mistakes is growing compassion and kindness within me, which naturally brings more laughter and ease into our home."

Louise Sevigny
Kid Code Teacher
Co-Owner, Your Good Company, Ltd.

Kindness and Mental Health

(Excerpt from CMHA)

Never get tired of doing little things for others,
sometimes those little things occupy the
biggest parts of their hearts.
—Unknown

The Canadian Mental Health Association (CMHA) has this to say about how kindness and helping others affects our mental health:

Helping others feels good! When you help others, it promotes positive physiological changes in the brain associated with happiness.

Helping others improves social support, encourages us to be more physically active, distracts from our problems, and allows us to engage in meaningful activity.

Sense of belonging & reduces isolation: Face to face activities can reduce loneliness and isolation.

It Helps Keep things in Perspective: different perspectives can impact our outlook on life.

Helping others in need can provide us with perspective and allow us to appreciate what we have.

It's Contagious! Acts of Kindness have the potential to make the world happier and improve confidence, control, and optimism.

The More You Do for Others, the More You Do for Yourself: Evidence shows that the benefits of helping others has long lasting affects by providing a "kindness bank" of memories.

It Reduces Stress: Positive emotions reduce stress and boost our immune system.

It Can Help Us Live Longer: Giving and helping others may increase how long we live. Evidence shows that those who give support live longer than those who don't.

Kindness & Mental Health. P 2. Date accessed: May 07, 2021. (https://novascotia.cmha.ca/wp-content/uploads/2018/05/MHAW.pdf)

To live longer, bless mistakes!
To be happier, bless mistakes!
To reduce stress, bless mistakes!
To feel good, bless mistakes!

CHAPTER 3

Natural or Nasty

By being natural and sincere, one can create revolutions
without having sought them.
—Christian Dior

What's Natural?

One day all I could feel was love, and it landed on everything in its path, without prejudice. It landed on my thumbnail, on the blade of grass, on the bird poop on the deck. I'd missed what is rather obvious: It's so great that birds can poop. It would be so awful if they couldn't. They'd die. I had previously not been overjoyed to clean up the bird poop on the deck. Since that day, I've been grateful for so much, even that birds can poop, and I'm alive to clean it up! If that sounds strange, I've never been saner in my life. Once gratitude and Grace have visited you in this way, you realize you have everything backwards if you don't love what creation has created.

This love rested on the store clerk who was frowning at me. Love was the state of being, and it rendered me joyful and harmless. It landed on every single human being in front of me. It was Grace. Those states have come to me quite a few times, and I'm always reminded that when they do, I feel 100 percent natural.

During the times Grace was my CEO, I couldn't have hurt a fly or an ant or another human being. I realized that was my natural state. It worked really well for me and for those around me. I didn't want anything from anyone, and they were safe with me.

The next time I judged another person or punished someone with criticism, I wanted to cry because it was so far from what was natural to me—and you.

Punishing the other feels awful inside us, so it
is punishing us.
Prove that to yourself by noticing how you feel
when you punish another person when he or she makes a mistake.
Compassion is natural to us.

Kids Teach Us What Comes Naturally and What Doesn't Because We've Forgotten

Kids teach us
what they want us to teach them.

Kids are in their natural states most of the time. That's largely why they are so lovable and irresistible. And we're not in our natural states most of the time, and that's what makes us a little bit hard to love and easy to resist.

In any of the following states that feel natural, there is never anything wrong, and we care for everyone. These are pure emotions.

Natural States of a Human Being (as taught by children):

- Inclusive (They play with anyone who will play with them.)
- Without prejudice (They don't register body size, skin color, perceived status.)
- Joyful for no reason (As Byron Katie says!)
- Curious
- Lighthearted
- Compassionate
- Belly-laughing
- Spontaneous
- Creative (They can play wholeheartedly with a stick, some rocks, and a cardboard box for hours.)
- Genuine
- Supportive
- Accepting
- Loving
- Inspired
- At ease

That is our Essential or True Nature too.
Kids are teaching us this.

During an upset, our natures are like the sun
when it is hidden behind clouds.
It's still there, but we can't see it. (Sadhguru)

In that way, our belly laughs,
Playfulness, and all other natural states are not gone.

Living life in these ways works because it's natural to us. Punishing isn't on the list because it's not part of our natures. Punishing is what we learned, so we can unlearn it.

What Is Nasty (Unnatural, Not in Our Natures)

*As long as your mind with its conditioned patterns
runs your life, what choice do you have? None.*
—Eckhart Tolle

Imagine our minds as icebergs. Upsetting emotions are stored in the bottom of our icebergs—the unconscious mind—and rise to the top of our icebergs—the conscious mind—under certain conditions.

The first temper tantrums we had is still stored in the bottoms of our icebergs. Those emotions (the tantrum type) come up when they're nudged awake by something we want that we don't get. They are there in the first place because we misidentify with things like, "If I get that [meaning anything we want], I'll be whole, happy, right, settled, and so on." When we don't get what we want, the emotions rise in an attempt to help us get what we want. Except, they can't help us. Notice this for yourself. In an upset state you can't help yourself or another—ever.

Emotions *are thoughts* on steroids. For example, when this is the thought: "I want that," and I don't get it, anger, frustration, worry, and so on arise. The emotion comes up because the thought, *I want that*, gets stronger.

The whole mess happens because we are attached to or identified with a thought. If we're not attached or identified, we don't overreact. These are conditioned patterns that we learned at the same time we learned to have a tantrum, and they can be dissolved with some dedicated work.

We can be consumed by these negative emotions and behaviors, or we can operate by our natural, pure emotions, which are always harmless and always joyful. Pure emotions don't *want* anything. They are a natural part of us, like we see in kids. They are not stored in the bottoms of our icebergs; they are part of who we are.

Dr. Joe Dispenza, whose postgraduate training includes neuroscience, teaches, "Where your attention goes, your energy flows." When we put our attention on a negative state, it grows. He is pointing to this: If we feel negative and put our attention on that state, it operates us now and gets more established to operate us later.

Through scientific testing, Dr. Dispenza has demonstrated that emotions are addictive. We learn something negative, and we remember, just like we learned and remembered our ABCs. The thoughts become emotions that "fire and wire together" as our icebergs' operating systems and negative thoughts and emotions become second nature to us. This means a negative emotion is a chemical reaction from the past. It also means negative emotions are not parts of our natures, so they can be dissolved. That's a good reason to pay attention to dissolving these states when they arise instead of letting them settle back to the bottom of our icebergs to arise another day and cause us misery.

Later in the book you will find several exercises for exorcising these upsetting ways of living in the world:

- Fearful
- Worrying
- Sad
- Angry

- Unhappy
- Disappointed
- Troubled
- Perturbed
- Unsettled
- Dismayed
- Offended
- Distressed
- Anxious
- Confused
- Disgusted
- Overwhelmed
- Pessimistic
- Petty
- Controlling
- Punishing
- Full of pretense

We never feel natural in these states, which proves they are not part of our natures. Every time we feel or act out one of these states, it's just a mistake. Remind yourself, "I matter more than the mistake of behaving this way." And then make the mistake right by apologizing and doing whatever is necessary for you to feel good inside.

Upset or Uplifted?

Problems are not stop signs,
they are guidelines.
—Robert H. Schuller

There is no good reason for an upset. We often get upset with others' mistakes, and for sure, we get upset every time one of our beliefs is challenged. I started to wonder if upsets were helpful in any way.

Did they ever help with my well-being?

One day I called my dad to tell him about a family crisis before he heard it from someone else. Someone had made a mistake that hurt another person in my family. I was crying, and he said, "You've got fifteen minutes to be upset." I went on sniffling and pointing out what was wrong. He patiently listened, without commenting.

After I'd gone on for ten minutes, he said, "You have five minutes left."

Then, I laughed out loud because I sensed another lesson was coming and I'd just wasted ten minutes in negativity. Although it's never a waste if it's attached to a life-altering lesson.

"You'll be no good to your child or to yourself if you stay upset," he said. I caught what he taught. My dad turned my upset into an uplift.

Since that day, I've been looking for a good reason to be upset when something goes "wrong," or someone makes a mistake. I still get upset, but I notice right away that there is not a good reason to be upset. So I bless myself and all others involved.

Then my insides soften, and my heart takes over, I feel reverence and gratitude for life. Confusion fades, and clarity appears. I value all of life. It's a beautiful feeling.

There is no good reason to be upset
when a mistake is made.

Being upset is not good
for our well-being.

How Did We Get Offtrack, Away from Our Natures?

Your unhappiness ultimately arises not from
the circumstances of your life,
but from the conditioning of your mind.
—Eckhart Tolle

As children, we learned and then unconsciously adopted ideas or beliefs that we falsely thought promised us success, safety, health, and happiness. If we examine them, we realize they cause stress, not success.

For example, if we saw a parent, caregiver, sibling, relative, or family friend criticizing another person while insisting they're right, implying they are better than the one they are criticizing, that's what we learned and adopted. As a child, we don't even know the words, yet we absorb the belief. Then it becomes an unconscious, pain-causing go-to.

They are implying, "I'm right to criticize others because I am better than they are."

Except that doesn't do any good, *and* it doesn't feel good inside us to criticize another person. We actually feel stress when we criticize others. Once we notice that, we won't want to do it as often. Once we realize it doesn't really keep us safe, happy, healthy, or successful, we can let it go instead of letting it be our go-to.

Anything that's true
we don't need to change.

Everything that's not true
we need to see, so we can change.

Beliefs Unveiled

Taking responsibility for your beliefs and judgments
gives you the power to change them.
—Byron Katie

Where did you learn your beliefs? It's likely they were learned from parents, siblings, the community, school, religion, friends, authorities, governments, and spiritual leaders.

The key word is "learned." They are not part of our natures. That's proof beliefs are *not* who we are and not truths just because we learned them. Here's an example.

> GRANDDAUGHTER: "Grama, I'm so upset. I made an excuse instead of doing what I needed to."
>
> ME: "If you get quiet, can you see what you gained by making an excuse?"
>
> GRANDDAUGHTER: "Yes, it's ... if I make an excuse, I'll be free."
>
> ME: "That's the learned belief. Your formula for freedom is to make an excuse. We have all believed that at one time or another, and we can't help it until we 'see' it. Can you see how it operates you?"
>
> GRANDDAUGHTER: "It's a loop that keeps running. I want to be free, so I make an excuse. I make an excuse to get myself free. Ugh, Grama."
>
> ME: "Can you see where you learned this idea?"
>
> GRANDDAUGHTER: "Yes, it was ..." (She named a specific event she experienced as a child.)

ME: "So it's clear that you learned the belief. I asked you where you learned it, and you could see the specific event. Beliefs are learned. All of us learn them from our families and our cultures, and we couldn't have done it differently. Nor could our families or our cultures because they learned it from someone who learned it from someone else."

"Do you believe that idea now that you've done the work—'Excuses make me free'?"

GRANDDAUGHTER: "No, it doesn't work. Excuses don't set me free. They get me in trouble."

ME: "What if that idea wasn't your unconscious operating system?"

GRANDDAUGHTER: "I'd never make an excuse, so I could set myself free."

ME: "So when something needs doing, it could just get done. This belief/operating system wouldn't create the pain of not doing it and making an excuse to be free?"

GRANDDAUGHTER: "Yes."

ME: "That's proof that if you didn't have the belief, there would be no upset. The upset is caused by the belief itself. This is how it unconsciously operates you. You want to feel free, so don't do what needs doing, and then you make an excuse and feel free. If that belief—which is learned and doesn't work—isn't in your unconscious mind, you can't be operated by it. You can be operated by your True Nature, which doesn't believe anything that isn't true.

GRANDDAUGHTER: "Grama, did you write that down?"

My heart melts all over myself when my grandkids understand the truth.

Poking Holes in Beliefs: Proof the Punishment Paradigm Is Flawed

Insight allows us to safely change to what the heart knows is right and true.

Punishing another human being is punishing ourselves. While we're doing it, we feel bad; if we do something that makes us feel bad, that's punishing ourselves.

We often punish another person or give them grief when a mistake is made. There is a more peaceful way to coexist. Blessing another's mistake is a blessing for them and for us.

The following logic challenges common beliefs about punishment when someone makes a mistake as a way to change behavior. This logic can be used as a reminder any time we want to punish anyone for any reason.

Ubuntu, restorative justice and blessing mistakes are examples of more effective ways to change behavior. Try them and see.

1. Common belief: *Spare the rod and spoil the child.*
   a. If we don't punish them, they will be spoiled.
      i. To ensure good behavior in others we must show bad behavior—punish someone.
   b. Punishing the other means *we* are good people if it makes the one who is punished become good.
      i. Good people are punishers.
      ii. Those who punish are good people. Really? Do we think that when we see someone punish a dog? "That's a good person, right there, the one hitting the dog." If we know it's not right to hit a dog, we know it's not right to hit a child. We inherently know it's not right to punish, we just don't know another way, yet.

"Bless me for believing that punishing another person makes me a good person. I matter more than that mistake. I can make it right by noticing when I'm punishing myself or another human being and ask if I could myself to stop."

2. Common belief: *A spanking never hurt anyone.* (Bend over, and we'll see.)
   a. Connect with the indignity and feeling that you should be punished.
   b. Does humiliating someone cause well-being?
   c. When we're punished, we draw the conclusion, "I am bad—otherwise, they wouldn't do this to me." That imprints on us deep inside. We constantly try to rid ourselves of this, yet at the same time, it's something we live by.
   d. Just a minute ago we said punishment makes the other into a good person. Here we are saying we make people feel bad by punishing them. See the contradiction?
   e. When we're punished, we conclude that we must not be worthy. Spanking hurts more than the bum. Punishment doesn't make good people; it makes people feel unworthy.

"Bless me for believing two contradictory beliefs. I didn't know I was believing those things. I matter more than the mistake. I can make it right by noticing how I feel inside when I'm punishing someone and stop and apologize."

3. Common belief: *They need to learn a lesson.*
   a. That means learning is aided by punishment.
   b. Punishment is a good teacher.
   c. What lessons do they learn?
      i. How to punish themselves and others.

"Bless me for believing that I am teaching someone when I'm punishing them. I matter more than the mistake. I can make it right by blessing mistakes instead of punishing mistakes and seeing for myself which is the better teacher."

4. Common belief: *That's how it's done, so it must be all right.*

    a. Or might it cause lasting damage that goes underground, only to resurface in us as anger, impatience, frustration, bullying, and anxiety for the rest of our lives?

"Bless me for believing that just because a society has adopted a strategy—that it's right. I can make my actions right by critical thinking, by checking to see if I feel peaceful while I act out the role of punisher, and by using my own inner bliss barometer. How do I feel when I punish myself or another person? If I don't feel good inside, I'm being operated by a belief taught by society that isn't true."

These beliefs cause us stress.
They don't make our lives easier or better.
They beliefs can't deliver what they promise.

Blessing a mistake causes us peace.
It makes our lives easier and better.
It can deliver what it promises: respect and connection.

These common beliefs are not true so far, yet we go on thinking and acting as though they are.

None of these beliefs cause long-term happiness, yet we go on thinking and acting as though they will.

None of these beliefs can assure success, yet we go on thinking and acting as though they will.

True success is inner well-being that can't be shaken by anything going on in the outer world.

Everyone wants happiness.
Everyone wants less stress.

Since that's true, it's time to regularly examine, upset by upset, the *cause* of upsets so we can free ourselves of letting upsets define us and relax back into our naturally happy states.

And we need to understand the true *cause* of happiness so we can get more of it.

One way to have more happiness and less stress is to practice blessing mistakes on a mistake-by-mistake basis!

Beliefs are never going to cause happiness. Kids don't believe any of those things until we teach them. They are naturally happy without the need for beliefs. It's monkey-see, monkey-do with kids. That's how they adopt beliefs that don't serve them.

Do kids need to believe anything to put their little hand in yours, or does it come naturally? Do they need to believe before they can be creative, or does it come naturally? Connection is natural to them, and they don't need a belief to make it true. Do kids need to assess who they play with before they play with someone, or does play come naturally?

We believe that what we believe will make us happy, successful, healthy, and safe. It makes us stressed-out, selfish, and unhappy. It also makes us physically, mentally, and emotionally sick.

With any belief, we never feel natural; we feel the opposite of natural. Beliefs cause us to feel uncomfortable in our own skin. That sends us looking for something to make us feel better (shopping, gossiping, addictions) and the cycle, the no-exit loop continues: trying for and failing at finding long-term happiness.

A belief mandates an idea we then have to live up to: live it, support it, and finally, suffer it. That ensures we stay out of our essential selves, and stay glued to looking to the outer world for happiness. We hang on to false ideas to fulfill us. (A new car will make me happy—until someone bangs their door into it in the parking lot; until we have to pay for it, until we have to fix it when it breaks down.)

We live under clouds while the sun shines brightly behind them.

Our essential natures don't need beliefs to live joyfully. When we feel natural, we know what to say and do without any thinking involved— just like kids do. If we grow up with these truths, our wisdom and compassion develop further instead of being obscured.

Beliefs cause stress and punish us. Uncovering them dissolves them and what's left is what's natural.

The Grief Gremlin

Be an encourager. The world
has plenty of critics already.
—Unknown

This is what is really happening when we give ourselves or another grief. First, we feel bad. The next time you punish someone or give another grief physically (pushing, hitting, and so on), with words (judging, criticizing), with actions (take actions that will hurt another person like taking something that's theirs), or have bad thoughts about the person, check and see how you feel inside yourself. You will likely notice how awful you feel.

Giving the other grief takes us
out of our own states of well-being.
"Bless me for that mistake, I didn't know."

The feelings worsen as we defend, justify, and make excuses that we're right, and that the one we've punished is wrong. Watch for how you feel inside as you defend, justify, and make excuses for yourself. We don't feel good in the moment we defend, etc. Noticing this gives us insight into ourselves that we can find in no other way. "Hey, I've never noticed that while I'm making excuses, I really don't feel good inside. I wonder if that indicates something."

"Defending or making an excuse
never serves our own well-being.
"Bless me, I didn't know."

Assess the relationship in the moment you give another grief. It's likely not good. Everyone is tense, stressed out, and disconnected.

"I had no idea that I'm not paying attention to
what causes trouble in a relationship.
Bless me, I didn't know."

The False Promise of Punishment

Extreme justice is often injustice.
—Jean Racine

Those who have been punished:

Learn how to punish themselves and others. They have a "how-to" manual after being punished and will pass that on, along with their hair and eye colors, when they have kids.

Learn that they are bad, and then start to live down to that.

Learn that they are not good enough.

Learn that the way to relate to others is to punish them.

Learn that having been bullied and punished allow them to seek others who are insecure and then bully them.

Learn that addiction, due to the self-punishing policy they've unconsciously adopted, is the solution to feeling bad. And they don't know how they got there.

Correction vs. Punishment

Never miss a good chance
to shut up.
—Will Rogers

A correction:

- Has no negative energy behind it.
- Is a sharing of what works to connect in relationships/life.
- Is a sharing of what doesn't work to connect in relationship/life.
- Has no blame. It doesn't need blame as karma takes care of actions with natural consequences.
- Explains what naturally happens with certain behaviors. If we're talking to children, it's good to, with loving compassion, ask them to notice how they feel inside when they're upset, and share that it is not good for their well-being.

If you feel like punishing someone mentally by criticizing, belittling, devaluing, or judging words, or physically, do the quick coherence technique that follows to get yourself back into a clear-thinking place.

In a clear, coherent state, I find it impossible to be anything but loving toward myself and another human being. Punishment becomes impossible, and correction is welcomed.

"Bless me.
I matter more than the mistake
I've made by punishing people.
I will make it right to each of them where I can."

Coherence

Blessing mistakes is a coherence-creating state. But in the beginning, or even as you progress to living a calmer life, there are times when a little extra help is a good idea. HeartMath is scientifically proven to help bring about peace and coherence. This is what I like to call 'peace and quiet'.

This simple technique helps us regulate our stressful, emotionally charged, and energy-draining situations.

HeartMath Quick Coherence® Technique

The Quick Coherence® technique was developed by and is a registered trademark of HeartMath (https://www.heartmath.com).

> Create a coherent state in about a minute with the simple, but powerful steps of the Quick Coherence® Technique. Using the power of your heart to balance thoughts and emotions, you can achieve energy, mental clarity and feel better fast anywhere. Use Quick Coherence® especially when you begin feeling a draining emotion such as frustration, irritation, anxiety or anger. Find a feeling of ease and inner harmony that's reflected in more balanced heart rhythms, facilitating brain function and more access to higher intelligence.

The Technique

> Step 1: Focus your attention in the area of the heart. Imagine your breath is flowing in and out of your heart or chest area, breathing a little slower and deeper than usual.

> Suggestion: Inhale 5 seconds, exhale 5 seconds (or whatever rhythm is comfortable).

> Step 2: Make a sincere attempt to experience a regenerative feeling such as appreciation or care for someone or something in your life.

> Suggestion: Try to re-experience the feeling you have for someone you love, a pet, a special place, an accomplishment, etc. or focus on a feeling of calm or ease.

What Is Coherence, and Why Does It Matter?

A simple definition of coherence is that it is a state that is orderly, harmonious, and makes sense. Another is capable of intelligent perception, speech, thought, and actions.

Why is coherence important?

Incoherence happens when we are:

- under pressure
- feeling stressed out
- feeling anxious
- reactive instead of responsive
- feeling fearful, worried, angry, sad, and unable to think straight.

Coherence is the state of being in which we are able to:

- Feel refreshed and invigorated.
- Feel relaxed, even with deadlines.
- Feel all our natural states: compassion, joy, inclusivity, belly laughing, playful, loving, and so on.
- Experience clarity.

Coherence is our natural state. That's why we are brought back to it with any strategy we use to dissolve stress.

> Blessing mistakes is one way to
> bring ourselves back into coherence.

I Use Blessing Mistakes for Almost Anything

"The Blessing Mistakes tool has become a staple in our family's daily operations.

I started using it on frustrating little blunders my kids would make, like spilling things or breaking something. I immediately noticed a difference in my interactions with them. It was a way for me to circumvent the frustration that usually boiled up during these common occurrences.

While I valued having a tool that would help get through these situations, I will never forget the day that I really learned just how important blessing a mistake could be. I was having a "day"; my kids were not cooperating, I was late, everything that could go wrong was going wrong. I lost it on my kids. I yelled, was rude, angry, and way overreactive.

One of those times where you could actually see the damage of my behavior right on my kids' faces. I dropped them off at school and immediately called my sister. Once I unloaded the events of the morning on her (which we do every now and then when it feels like too much, mostly just lending an ear), she was quiet, and then she said, "Bless you." I felt so much relief in that moment.

From then on, I use the tool for almost everything. When my kids are in a bad mood, when they are acting out against someone else, when they have done something they regret, when they are embarrassed about something. There are endless situations where this tool can be used. It eases the tension of any situation so practical action can be taken, and the situation can be handled in a calm manner.

I am very grateful for this tool. I highly recommend giving it a try."

Amanda Miller
(Full disclosure: Amanda is my daughter)
BSc, RMT, Certified Lifeprint Analyst and Instructor
Kid Code Teacher

Sour Lemons

When life gives you lemons
order the lobster tail!
—Ziad K. Abdelnour

There is a common fallacy that life gives us lemons. What give us lemons is what we think and believe about what happens in our lives. That's good news because we can change what we think and believe. We often can't change what happens in life.

For example, we can't change the following:

- Aging.
- Others' big emotions.
- Others' unconscious actions.
- The weather.
- Government/corporations/organizations actions or inactions.

What we believe about them makes us sour. They are going to go on doing what they do whether we are sour or not.

Here's the short version of how lemons appear in our lives. As little kids, we adopt certain ideas that we think will keep us safe, healthy, happy, and successful. But these ideas don't work. Look around, you don't know one person who is in those states all the time. That's proof that what we learned isn't working.

We don't realize that what we learned as children is still guiding us and still doesn't work to cause unshakable success, which is another way to say feeling good on the inside of us no matter what's going on—on the outside of us.

For example, "If I am a good girl, then people will approve of me and that will make me happy and successful." Look at all the approval we've gotten—and we still strive for more. Believing I'm a good girl can't cause long-term happiness. Being natural does that. Since being a good girl can't cause long-term happiness, it gives us lemons. If you sit quietly with "I'm a good girl," it will make you mad or sad, or maybe both. Prove this sour-making thought to yourself.

Being good comes naturally to us without seeking approval from others to prove it, and oddly, when we're natural, that gains everyone's approval even though, at that point, we don't need or want it.

'Sour lemons' is such a good fallacy, I'd like to use it.

> If life gives us lemons with which to make lemonade, how long should we keep them sour before we make them sweet?
>
> Staying sour is the opposite of coherence. Keeping sour lemons sour causes a lot of stress.
>
> Blessing mistakes makes lemons into sweetness!

What Is Stress, and What's the Problem with It?

Stress let's break up.
—Unknown

Stress is a feeling of tension. When it's a natural response, it's good because stress chemicals kick in to move us physically out of danger. But it's important the stress chemicals dissipate as soon as they are not needed. Dr. Joe Dispenza says we spend 70 percent of our day in a state of stress.

We've falsely, and often unconsciously, think that being stressed out will benefit us. We'll get things done, others will help us, others won't hurt us, and so on. At the same time, we desperately want to live without stress.

Dr. Dispenza explains that we can turn on the stress response and stress chemicals, "by thought alone." How many stressful thoughts do we have in a day? He adds that we can't live in an emergency state for an extended period of time. Stressful thoughts equal disease.

The stress chemicals wreak havoc with our bodies and minds. This is not new information, but it's not information that we act on regarding our well-being. Getting rid of stress as a daily priority changes our emotional, physical, and mental health. Dr. Joe Dispenza, *The Danger With Prolonged Stress. 1:51.* August 14, 2020. Accessed March 15, 2021. (https://www.youtube.com/watch?v=3Bfbbh7UqDY)

Blessing mistakes gets rid of stress!

CHAPTER 4

The Invitation from Grace to Release All Useless Blockages to Joy

How to Get Back on Track: Exorcise the Upsets

> *Who you are is not an option.*
> *You are love.*
> —Byron Katie

When we are outside our True Natures we feel upset.

When we're in our True Natures we feel at ease.

Another name for upsets, troubles, challenges, adversities, and so on, is

Grace.

That's because in the moment we feel upset, we are caught in a belief, or in wrong thinking, and that caused the stress we experience. Grace has given us the awareness of the upset to guide us back to right thinking.

Life itself doesn't want us to feel bad. Life wants us to feel alive. No negative state feels alive in a good way.

An upset is an invitation to see the real cause of and cure for our wrong thinking and stress. As soon as we see a belief, we have an aha moment, which is also

Grace.

The upset and the aha are both Grace.

The Upset Is Inevitable: How We Handle It Determines Our Ongoing Level of Peace

As Guy Finley teaches, beliefs are preexisting, having been adopted in childhood, so the moment of overreaction is inevitable. That means you can't stop the upset. What we can stop is the continuation of it, letting it think, speak, and act for us. Over time, with this work, upsets are less frequent and have less intensity. Until deeper core beliefs arise, the upsets are intense. But once they've cleared, the peace we experience is even deeper.

There are a few exercises that are offered to you throughout the book that are repeated. You are encouraged to do them every time they appear. Each exercise you do, even if you've done it before, will remove layers of conditioning and help you feel more and more free.

Catch the Upset
If you don't catch the upset, it will catch you. That means you will feel upset and miserable instead of natural and clear.

Here is a list of things you can say and/or do that can help to stop you from being carried along by the emotional upset:

- Imagine a big stop sign in front of your face. This indicates it's time to stop yourself from being dragged away by an overreaction.
- "I don't want to feel like this."
- "This will cause me misery."
- "This will hurt others."
- "I need to unfriend this part of me."
- "Blocking the identity now."
- "I see you" (said to the identity).
- "I'm about to agree to make myself miserable."
- "I'm about to get irrational while thinking I'm smart and right."
- Put your hand over your mouth so the identity cannot speak.

- Put your hand over your heart and ask for your essential nature to take over as CEO.
- Look up and ask for divine intervention: "Divinity, I need an intervention!"
- Stop midsentence when you begin to feel uncomfortable.
- Put the full force of your attention on your breathing, in and out (Eckhart Tolle), and don't waver until you feel calm enough to look inward at the cause of the upset.
- "Something I learned in childhood is about to make my life miserable."
- "Help!" Imagine calling the fire department, wanting to put this fire out before it destroys everyone in its path.
- "SOS"—save our sanity. We are in an emergency state if we're about to be taken over and run by something that will hurt everyone, including ourselves.
- "You can't have me" (said to the identity).
- "You think you can help, but you can only harm" (said to the identity).
- Imagine a, "Y in the road"' (Guy Finley), and make a conscious choice about which path you want to take. When we teach this to kids we say, "You get to choose Happy Street or Mad Street." Or you can teach kids to say this or say it yourself, "You're not the boss of me" (said to the negative emotion).
- "Why am I going along with this insanity?"
- "I don't need this anymore."
- "This overreaction will do me no good."

Use Guy Finley's suggestion. He says—sort of tongue in cheek, but he also means it, and he's right—the two most spiritual words you'll ever hear are: shut up and you only say them to yourself. Louise Sevigny, a Kid Code teacher, says the polite Canadian version, said to ourselves is, "Be quiet, please." If we are able to be quiet instead of talking and watch the identity and its accompanying painful emotions into obscurity, we won't get ourselves in so much hot water with others!

If you feel upset because someone has made a mistake and felt the good feeling of blessing them but negativity seeps back in later, these strategies will help you feel better. And they only take a few minutes.

You are invited to try them all and then work with the ones that you resonate strongly with.

To end an upset or dismiss a negative thought after you've blessed the person's mistake but still feel a bit "off," you are invited to give yourself coherence and return to your nature by using any of these techniques. Before beginning this work, reminding yourself of the following ideas will help you to understand and make your inner work easier:

— Doing this exercise doesn't excuse the other person for his or her behavior. It just frees us from reacting and behaving in a negative way. We may have to do it several times on several occasions to clear the negativity because it's been our go-to programming.

— Their behavior is about them. They could do no differently believing what they did/do in the same way when we overreact. We couldn't do any differently because we were believing what we were believing, which dictated our words and actions.

— Don't take the behavior they direct at you personally. They mistakenly believe something that makes them act or speak in the ways they do. Remember what Jack Canfield says; they would do the same to anyone.

— "The upset is not a natural part of me. The upset is striking my reactive identity."

— "My reaction is about me, and I want to come from a calmer place."

— "If I wasn't somehow attached to_____ [insert the negative state you're in], the whole thing would run off me like water off a duck's back."

- "If I engage or entangle, feel even the slightest upset, it's a sign that I can do this simple strategy to get right now relief and come back into my True Nature. I have that power."
- "I want to live from my True Nature, not from upsetting beliefs and identities that cause upsetting thoughts and emotions that lead me to speak and act poorly."

It's helpful to get quiet; take slow, deep breaths; close your eyes; and ask your body to relax before you do these strategies. If your body feels fidgety, you can start at your feet, and invite them to relax and get still. Work your way up until you feel relaxed.

Don't judge yourself or the other. Just do the exercises and see what happens.

Feel It Flee
Summarize your upset in a word or two (or a few).

> I'm upset because he was _____ (rude, for example) to me. The word "rude" becomes the focus. Feel what that word brings up in you until it passes. This dissolves the emotion and belief to whatever extent it can because seeing it and feeling it are done consciously.

I Am That
Ask to see:

> Where was I rude (using rude as an example) anytime to anyone?

> Wait quietly to be shown. We all have all behaviors; some are more prominent in us, and some are less prominent. An image or memory of a time you were rude will come. Feel the uncomfortable feelings that arise until they pass, taking with them the attachment to rudeness.

Ask to see:

> Where did I learn that rudeness was good, that it appeared to achieve something positive? What event taught me this? Look into your childhood, and quietly wait for an answer. You may recall a sibling acting rudely, and a parent laughing at it. The idea that was adopted is rudeness is funny. Experience the feelings that arise until they pass, taking with them the attachment to rudeness.

It's Already Healed (As Taught by Gregg Braden, a spiritual teacher)
While I understand him to be teaching this for physical healing, we'll use it for healing upsets caused by identification because it works.

- Get quiet.
- Give the upset a word or phrase. Usually, you notice it in another person, which is the indicator that you are attached. Don't judge; just do it.
- Say to yourself, "It's already healed."
- Feel as though the healing has happened, that the upset no longer has control over you.
- Feel gratitude for being healed.

> Upsets and negativity are not part of our nature, so in effect, they don't exist except in our minds. That's how we're already healed. Our natures have no negativity in them, so we are already healed from being negative.

Stay on the Launchpad
My longtime inner-work buddy, Lesia, came up with this moniker for the work that follows. It means when you feel the upset, stay with it, don't launch yourself at another person or into ranting and raving, defending, justifying, making excuses, lying, avoiding, fighting, and so on.

Eckhart Tolle teaches that if we are aware, we'll feel the upset/emotion first in the body. As soon as you feel it, stay on the launchpad. Take no action; speak no words. Defer to feeling the emotions and sensations fully until they pass. With this exercise, there is no need to name the upset. Just feel it until it passes.

Using the External to Calm the Internal
Once you have gotten hold of yourself and are still on the launchpad, you can do the following to further weaken the identity/attachment/false self and bring yourself into coherence.

- Put your full attention and focus on you and everything around you—the air, the trees, the floor, the walls, and so on (as taught by Eckhart Tolle).
Put your full attention and focus on something in nature until calmness arises.

All the World's a Stage
Put your full attention and focus on becoming the observer, the watcher, by mentally stepping behind, stepping back from what's happening. Watch what the identity/attachment thinks, says, and acts out until calmness arises.

Image you are two people. Leave the upset one onstage and take the other curious you behind the scenes to watch the upset as it acts out.

Feel the Inner Body (Eckhart Tolle)
This is one way to come back to your inner nature and disempower the upset. Put your full attention and focus on the inner self. Start by feeling the energy in your hands or feet. Move through the body, feeling the inner energy.

What's the Gain?
If you can see the gain of believing a thought, you bring understanding to why you've been living the way you have. See what you gain by being

in the situation you are, by being treated the way you are and by being spoken to the way you are.

Sit quietly with your eyes closed and ask yourself, "What do I gain by this situation?" If you wait in silence, an answer will come. Some negative answers may come, but you can wait for a positive answer. That's the gain. For example, "When someone belittles me, what is it that I gain?" The answer for me was, "I'm better than they are." That's my identity, that's what I'm attached to. My formula for life is in order to be "better than," I need others to belittle me. How I (think) I make myself feel better than the other person is if they behave poorly and belittle me. Feeling this until it passes disempowers it.

This will reveal what's at the bottom of our icebergs (unconscious minds), driving us toward our personal *Titanic*.

Ho'oponopono
This is a popular Hawaiian ancient healing art with Polynesian roots that has been somewhat westernized and has a long and successful record. It means to "make it right." The goal is to release memories that are being manifest as problems. Do you know the story of Ho'oponopono and Dr. Hew Len? He cured twenty-nine out of thirty patients in a mental institution after only looking at their charts and repeating the Ho'oponopono words!

This is a wonderful clearing strategy. I have found several different versions of the wording and use the following one.

When the upset arises, say and feel each statement individually,

- I'm sorry.
- Please forgive me.
- Thank you.
- I love you.

Repeat until you feel natural.

"I Say 'Out'"

Louise Hay's strategy doesn't even entertain any identity by cutting it off as it arises: "I say, 'Out,' to every negative thought that comes to my mind. No person, place, or thing has any power over me, for I am the only thinker in my mind. I create my own reality and everyone in it."

Bless Yourself Over and Over

Keep blessing yourself for the mistake of feeling an old emotion right now and for the mistake of believing thoughts that are not helpful or true. Say and feel the truth of the statement, "I matter more than this mistake of being in this negative state."

Burn It Up

As mentioned in the Blessing Mistakes protocol to let a mistake go, Guy Finley invites us to feel the negative feelings burn up inside us. That means sit quietly and ask your inner wisdom to burn up this falseness. Wait until you feel a shift into peace.

The Results of Doing the Work

Notice the beautiful feeling of relief/release from the identity/attachment back into your True Nature. When we out of alignment with reality, with what's true, we are off-center and out of balance. Our thoughts, words, and actions will be off-center and out of balance as well.

If we're operated by a belief, we will have stress. If we're operated by what comes naturally to us, we will have happiness, ease, compassion, curiosity, playfulness, and be able to belly laugh.

Behaviors that are learned can be unlearned.
The pain they cause can be eliminated.

Unfriending Anger

For every minute you remain angry, you give
up sixty seconds of peace of mind.
—Ralph Waldo Emerson

Blessing mistakes is easier if we rid ourselves of some of the anger that keeps us from an act of kindness when someone makes a mistake. We all have some anger stored in us. How we know that is because every now and then, it rises *in* us.

We don't need it anymore.

Think of a situation when someone got angry at you. Get an image of them in your mind's eye.

> Notice they are convinced they are right while acting—a bit or a lot—insane.
> Notice they want what they want when they want it. The "I-ness" in their highness is present. Please bow, everyone!
> Notice they think they are establishing authority while appearing deranged.
> Notice their threatening voices and stances. Those are their strengths.
> Notice they think they are intelligent, though in the moment they are ranting, raving, and raging.
> Notice they think it will resolve the situation, bring solution, and therefore bring about peace and calmness. That's like saying anger will ultimately lead to soothing.
> Notice they think getting angry gets things done.
> Notice they think they have the right to direct their anger at others. They think they are entitled to get angry at others, but no one is entitled to get angry at them.
> Notice how arrogant they are.
> Notice that they are the judges, juries, and executioners.

Notice how they think they are exerting control by losing their own control.

Notice how powerful they think they are.

Notice how troubled and frantic they act.

Notice how much pain they are causing themselves.

Notice how ridiculous they look.

Notice how special they think they are and that they should get what they want. And when they don't, they get mad.

Notice that they think they are reasonable but are really just warring.

Notice they are bags of wind.

Notice an angry person thinks he or she is coming from a mentally superior position. In truth, the person is really coming from a mentally inferior position.

Notice that's us when we are angry.

Anger's True Signature

To me, habitual anger is like
sitting in a corner with a dunce cap on.
—Louise Hay

That visual alone could have a discouraging effect. Thank you, Louise.
—Lesia (my inner-work buddy)

GRANDDAUGHTER (AFTER DISCUSSING ANGER HER MIND HAD QUESTIONS ABOUT OTHER STATES THE MIND IS FOUND IN!): "Grama, if the family is having fun, is that our True Nature?"

ME: "Yes, when there is no negative charge, like when we're genuinely playful but we don't want anything from anyone else or the situation, that's our True Nature. At the same time, it's true that inner peace doesn't rely on outer events. Inner anger isn't caused by outer events either. They are both found inside. One causes us stress and the other is our True Nature."

GRANDDAUGHTER: "Grama, did you write that down?"

Pondering Anger

Try to find one good reason to be angry. I haven't found one. I'm still looking. Well-being can't be found near anger. Get weary enough of the anger to be willing to do the exercises to exorcise it.

Is it okay with you to be taken over by anger? If we don't dissolve the anger, we *are* agreeing to it.

Anger is hatred.
Anger puts my body, my relationships, and my well-being at risk.
Polishing my anger shrivels my heart.
Anger hemorrhages my energy.

Gratitude is the opposite of anger. Anger shuts down our immune systems. Gratitude improves it by 50 percent according to Dr. Joe Dispenza. If we dissolve our anger, what's left is gratitude.

As previously mentioned, Dr. Dispenza, who has studied and recorded his work with brain scans, says that we are in a stressed state 70 percent of the time. I wonder how much of that is spent in various states of anger from slight frustration and irritation all the way to raging.

Anger is a stressed state. Getting rid of it eliminates a lot of stress.

Become discontented with anger. Do you want anger to continue to inform your life? Something exists before and behind this anger. Find that.

True power is peaceful.
True peace is powerful.

Think of Mahatma Gandhi, Mother Teresa, Nelson Mandela, and Martin Luther King, Jr.

The Breaking Up Message

No one heals himself
by wounding another.
—Unknown

Use any one or a combination of these strategies when anger arises (some have been previously mentioned and are valuable here, also):

1. Don't judge yourself when you get angry. That hasn't worked and won't work.
2. Remove yourself from others before you react.
3. As John de Ruiter teaches, keep a note in your pocket that says, "I don't need my raging story anymore." Pull it out and read it every time anger arises.
4. Do your own inner work on the issue catalyzing the anger, using the methods offered in the previous section, or another self-inquiry method.
5. Use Ho'oponopono on the issue that catalyzes the anger, on the anger itself, or on any words that are upsetting: "I'm sorry." "Please forgive me." "Thank you." "I love you."
6. Silently step back from the anger. Watch it, and feel what it brings up.
7. Use Susi Lula, a self-care expert's, "I need a moment," strategy, and take it. See if you can stop anger in its tracks with one of these "I need a moment" ideas. Go into the next room, the bathroom, or anywhere, and focus on your breath. Do something physical; walk, run, garden, and so on.
8. Sit quietly in nature.
9. Remind yourself that anger won't get you what you want: peace, connection, compassion, real solutions, and so on.
10. Remind yourself you are about to, as Eckhart Tolle teaches, become confused/unclear and irrational.

11. Look at an angry person's face. Remind yourself that's what you look like when you're angry. Go look in the mirror when you're angry.

12. Remind yourself of what Sadhguru, a worldwide spiritual leader teaches. Getting angry is truly "mad," "insane." It's like taking poison and expecting the other person to hurt. Remind yourself getting angry causes damaging chemical reactions in the body. We're poisoning ourselves with our anger.

13. See if you can avert your attention and fully focus on following your breaths in and out for a few minutes. As taught by Eckhart Tolle, we can't think and follow our breaths at the same time.

14. Apologize to others. Explain that you are working on your anger issues and can see how damaging to relationships and useless it is.

For a proactive, deep dive into releasing anger, read each word on the very long and inclusive list at the end of this section. Close your eyes, and let the word bring up any uncomfortable feelings, images, or physical sensations that it does. Don't think it; feel it.

If you have trouble, the mind wants to chatter, and you just can't feel it, *invite yourself to focus on feeling it.* It is possible to feel anything here: physical, emotional, or mental pain or discomfort, which is caused by being attached to/identified with the concept you are working on. You might feel a slight pain in any area of your body, a tightening in the body, or anything at all. More than one emotion might arise. Feel any that do. A few different images of past or future traumas may arise.

If you still can't feel the feelings the word evokes, think of the feeling of the sun on your face and feel that. Then switch back to feeling the uncomfortable word. Remind yourself that you are doing this to free yourself of anger because it's not a natural part of you.

If you lose focus, remind yourself of the word you're working on. Then sink into focusing inside yourself. For example, inside your throat, and then broaden it to include the whole of the inside of you. Say to yourself, while you feel it, "I'm so sorry I'm attached to [insert the word you are working with]." Feel it until it lets go. You will feel a softening once the concept has been released, and the sensations that were present during the process will disappear. This releases whatever you are able to let go of at this time. You may be able to release more at another time. We build layers over time and we usually dissolve them in the same way. That's one reason the same emotion or issue comes up repeatedly for releasing.

Do as many words as you want in one sitting. Remember to do each word separately. Keep coming back to the list until you've gone through it completely. Each word may need to be felt for different lengths of time. It usually only takes a minute or two, but it could take more or less time. Some words will feel stronger and more painful than others. Take the time you need, and don't be afraid to go deep and dissolve as much as you can.

If the image of another person arises while you are doing this, bring your attention back to inside yourself, and keep feeling how this feels inside you. Clearing this in you can help clear it in others because we resonate with each other. But that's not the goal. If it doesn't clear it in others, at least we can be more peaceful when faced with their anger. The goal is to free ourselves of our anger and bring us back to feeling true inner well-being.

After you've done the complete word list once, do it again. The more you do it, the more you release.

And after the inner work is done, bless your mistake for reverting to anger as an old, ingrained, programmed habit. "I matter more the mistake of acting angry," and make it right with anyone you need to. If you like, you can say, "Goodbye _____(insert the word you're working on). I don't need you anymore."

The Word List

Abrupt, admonishing, affronted, aflame, aggravated, aggressive, angry, annoyed, antagonistic, apoplectic, argumentative, awful, bad-tempered, badgering, belligerent, beside myself, blazing, blistering, blustering, bothered, boiling, brusque, brutal, bullying, burning, cantankerous, castigating, caustic, censuring, chastising, cheesed off, cold, complaining, confrontational, contentious, crabby, cranky, critical, cross, cruel, curt, dangerous, defensive, defiant, demanding, difficult, disapproving, disciplining, discontent, disgruntled, displeased, disrespectful, dissatisfied, disturbed, edgy, enraged, exasperated, exasperating, explosive, fanatical, ferocious, fiery, foul, fractious, frenzied, frothing, fuming, furious, gnashing, goading, getting on my nerves, grouchy, grumpy, gunning for someone, harassing, harsh, hassling, hateful, heated, hopping mad, hostile, hotheaded, hounding, huffy, impatient, impudent, incensed, inciting, indignant, infuriated, insane (the angry kind), insistent, insolent, insulting, intolerant, irate, irking, irritable, irritated, justifying, livid, mad, moody, nagging, narrow-minded, objecting, offended, offensive, opinionated, ornery, out of sorts, outraged, passive-aggressive, peevish, penalizing, petulant, picky, piqued, prejudiced, prickly, provoked, provoking, pugnacious, punishing, punitive, pushy, put out, quarrelsome, rabid, raging, reactive, rebuking, rejecting, relentless, reprimanding, reproving, resentful, rigid, riled, rude, ruthless, sadistic, scalding, scorching, searing, seething, severe, sharp, short-tempered, slighting, smoldering, snappy, snippy, spitting mad, special (we get mad when someone doesn't treat us a special), spoiling for a fight, stern, stinging, strict, stubborn, surly, teed off, temper tantrumer, terrible, terse, testy, threatening, ticked off, touchy, truculent, uncompromising, unrelenting, up in arms, vehement, vexed, vexing, violent, witch-hunter, worked up, wound up, wrathful.

Can you bless yourself for the mistake of not doing this list completely until the anger ran out of you in rivers?

Resentment and Bitterness

There are no justified resentments
—Dr. Wayne Dyer

It always amazes me that I'm the only one hurting me when I hold resentment and bitterness about the past or towards another person. Why would I do that to myself? Will feeling resentment ever help me in any way? And how can it be true that there are no justified resentments? Because hurting myself over what someone else did or said *is not justified*.

Sit quietly and feel into each of these questions until you sense some release, and a new understanding or perspective frees you:

- Do I want to feel resentment and bitterness?
- Is there a good reason—even one good reason—for me to feel resentment and bitterness?
- Will it help me in any way if I feel resentment and bitterness?
- Is feeling resentment and bitterness relevant in this moment?
- Could I send love to that person who acted that way, so I can feel the feeling of love inside me instead of hate? (The prayer of St. Francis: "Where there is hatred, let me sow love.") Do this for your own sake.
- Could I bless myself for this mistake of harboring resentment and bitterness? "I matter so much more than this mistake of hurting myself by staying resentful and bitter."
- Could I bless the others for their mistakes? "_____ [name of the person who hurt you], "You matter so much more as a human being than your mistake does. I know you suffered when you made the mistake because I know I suffer when I make one."
- Could I bless myself for hurting others and making them feel resentment and bitterness? "I matter so much more than the mistake of hurting others."

Then, as best as you can, make all your mistakes right for your own well-being.

Release the Painful Past Since It's Not Here Now

Nothing happened in your past that can keep you from the present.
—Eckhart Tolle

We don't have to forget what's happened in the past—it's helpful to remember and not repeat what doesn't work.

It's painful for us if we don't forgive.

It's easier to bless our own and other's mistakes when we release our past traumas and the resentments that arise from the traumas.

Self-reflection sets us free of the pain of the past. When we let go, we surrender our false selves to our higher selves, and that is peaceful.

List every trauma, major upset, or crisis you ever experienced. Do one or two a day, or more, if it feels right for you. Journal about each of them. Include in each entry who was there, what they were doing, what their faces looked like, and what they did and said. What did you say and do? As you examine your list, include reflections such as:

- What feelings come up? Feel them until they dissolve. This dilutes your attachment to the event and dissolves the stored emotions.
- As you recall this event, what sights, smells, and sounds do you remember or experience?
- Notice that you are the one unable to feel compassion. What does this feel like? This moves us beyond resentment.
- What would it take for you to feel compassion for those that hurt you since they couldn't do any differently at the time due to their conditioning and beliefs?
- Could you forgive their mistakes for your own well-being? Bless their mistake. The human being that they are matters more than the mistake.
- Could you say, "I'm sorry for the mistake of hating someone?"

Think about the situation again. And if anything other than peace comes up, do the inquiry again. Each time more suffering will be released until you feel love toward the others.

I have witnessed the dramatic change in a person's inner state firsthand in classes all over the world when they do this type of inner work. It sets us free.

One student announced that he hated his mother because she tried to kill him. At the end of doing his work, he told the class he felt love for her. His nature had taken over, and his identification and attachment let go. That doesn't mean he will go near her. It means he doesn't have to suffer the hatred anymore. He was able to let go of the attachment, which is what this work is about. When we're not attached to an identity with upsetting emotions, we're in our natural loving states.

Format

Trauma: _____
Who was there; what did they say or do? _____
What did I say or do? _____
What feelings come up? _____
What images come up? _____
What sights, sounds, and so on come up? _____

Can I see my hatred right now?
I see that I am without compassion. Experience that. It feels really horrible that I can't be truly compassionate.
What would it take to feel compassion for _____ since they couldn't do any differently believing what they were believing?
Forgive them by blessing their mistake. This is for your well-being.

Example

Trauma: I see the semi in the oncoming lane moving into my lane. Cars are crashing into each other, people are dead, the baby has glass in her hair, the man is in shock and running across the highway.

Who was there, what did they say or do? My husband and kids and I, we were the last vehicle that didn't crash into one in front of it.

What did I say or do? I froze. Then I panicked.

What feelings come up? Intense fear. I feel it in my belly right now, years after it happened. I feel stunned. I'm shaking; my whole body is shaking.

What sights, sounds, and so on come up? It's sunny; we're in the mountains.

What images come up? I see me driving closer to the side of the road after this happens, I see me not feeling like I can trust semi-truck drivers. I get images being nervous in a vehicle when someone else is driving, I am reminded of this when I see a cutout in a hill that is similar to the one where the accident happened in the mountains. Tears come. I feel the hatred in me. It's a horrible feeling. It can't be natural.

I see that I am without compassion. I understand that he must be suffering so much for causing so many people's deaths. When I experience that, it feels really horrible that I can't be truly compassionate.

What would it take to feel compassion for the truck driver since he couldn't do any differently believing what he was believing? I wish he didn't have to suffer. That makes me feel better. I wish everyone didn't have to suffer. I forgive myself for not having compassion; I forgive him. Bless his horrible mistake. And mine.

Release comes, and I soften and feel compassion for all of us.

Next, list the times you've inflicted pain on and caused trauma to others.

Repeat the above exercise.

Format

Trauma I caused to another person: _____
Who was there; what did they say or do? _____
What did I say or do? _____
What feelings come up? _____
What images come up? _____
What sights, sounds, and so on come up? _____

Can I see my self-hatred right now?
I see that I am without compassion for myself. Experience that. It feels
really horrible that I can't be truly compassionate.

What would it take to feel compassion for myself since I couldn't do
any differently believing what I was believing?

"I matter more than the mistake of causing another person trauma, and
I have to make it right however I can."

Example:

Trauma I caused another person: I looked down on my mom when she
was sick.

Who was there, what did they say or do? Mom and I.

What did I say or do? I'm frowning at her, showing her my disapproval.

What feelings come up now? Sadness, disappointment in myself.

What images come up now? Her kind face, my unkind face. The tears
come to release me.

What sights, sounds, and so on come up? A quiet, sad silence.

I can feel the hatred, and let it keep itself alive as long as it can until it
passes, as it must, since it's not my nature.

What would it take to feel compassion for myself since I couldn't do any different, believing what I was believing? It's true that I didn't know any better, or I would have done better. How I know it's true that I didn't know any better is that I did it.

See that I am without compassion for myself. Experience that. It feels really horrible that I can't be truly compassionate. I feel the arrogance of thinking I shouldn't do things like that. That feels very painful.

Bless my mistake. I matter more than the mistake. I can't make it right to her because she's passed, but I can notice if I disapprove. And in her honor, I can stop myself, and do this work to clear disapproval out of me.

Release. Relief. Love and gratitude come. That's my nature. It feels natural.

CHAPTER 5

Teaching Kids Blessing Mistakes with Mr. Upalupagus's Secret Secrets

Excerpts from *Mr. Upalupagus's Secret Secrets*. Please note that some of the exercises learned in *Blessing Mistakes* are repeated in these stories. It can be helpful to do them again as they come up here (or many times— as many times as it takes to feel free!).

Preface

This is a bedtime—or anytime—storybook for kids and their:

- Parents
- Teachers
- Grandparents
- Caregivers
- Coaches

And everyone else who interacts with a child.

It teaches parents and kids:

- How to stay feeling joyful.
- How to de-stress when they move out of their natures.
- How to handle challenging people and situations—bullies, mistakes, sadness, anger, worry, fear, and so on.
- How to stay feeling genuinely curious, playful, spontaneous, generous, affectionate, forgiving, warmhearted, inclusive, nonjudgmental, accepting, connected, and how never to stop belly laughing.

Kids can also read it themselves anytime they have a problem they'd like to solve or to relieve an upsetting feeling they have inside. Or they can read it just for fun.

This book follows *The Kid Code 30 Second Parenting Strategies*, which teaches parents simple thirty-second strategies for peaceful and conscious, less-stressful parenting. The strategies give right now relief in an upset and raise awareness of how to calmly handle the challenges kids are guaranteed to bring.

During each story, your child is encouraged to include his or her favorite animal to experience the adventure and practice the "secret secrets." Or your family can choose an animal together.

The secret secrets are the strategies for staying or getting calm and joyful in any situation.

There is a note at the end of each story to help everyone learn, practice, and teach the secret secrets.

In the Beginning

There once was a wise, young elephant who roamed the plains of India, gathering other animal friends, and together, they became known as The Motley (that means assorted) Crew.

They came together to explore the outer world (go on adventures around the world) *and* to explore the inner world (how they feel inside of themselves) and stayed together because of a love for Mr. Upalupagus and his secret secrets, which made them feel lighter than "one thousand million" bubbles in a breeze.

Mr. Upalupagus is a lovable elephant because he loves everyone in every way—no exceptions.

He also knows the secrets of the Universe.

He is a bit different than others because he never gets upset—ever! He never has a frown, tears, or temper tantrums. Instead, he feels peaceful and playful. He says that's the natural way to be. It's okay if we're not that way though—we'll get there eventually. We can't be any different until we can. It's just that we feel bad when we're upset and that's no fun.

As a very young elephant, he learned the cause of, and the cure for, feeling upset.

Mr. Upalupagus is so wise that every time someone gets in trouble or feels bad, he knows of a simple way for them to make themselves feel *really* good. He calls them the secret secrets. When he's not with his Crew, you might see him meditating in the mountains, flying a helicopter, or playing baseball! Maybe you'll even see him and his Crew in your city, or in your backyard. You never know! Keep your eyes open!

The Motley Crew in Paris!

Note to parents and caregivers: Invite your child or your family as a whole to participate where indicated, or at any time during the stories!

Sparky the Dragon swooped through the sky, breathing fantastic friendly fire, and gracefully plunked herself down on the ground right beside the Crew. They were marching toward the city that brought up images of longing and love, and outdoor cafés aplenty in which to ponder those feelings.

Mama Llama was in heaven, dreaming about croissants and baguettes slathered with butter and saskatoon jam, walking along the Seine, and doing the cancan in Moulin Rouge.

King Cobra was beside himself with thoughts of Disneyland Paris!

But longing and love, and the sights in Paris, had nothing to do with what they were currently engaged in: trying to outshout each other about what to do in Paris. It sounded like the sky was falling.

As that thought crossed Sparky's mind, she remembered that Mr. Upalupagus had assured them that it was just a saying; the sky never really falls. That was good news for a dragon who loved to fly through it! In celebration, she breathed some more friendly fire! But she forgot to aim it at the sky, and she scorched the earth a tiny bit! Oops.

"Oh, no, look what I did to the earth!" cried Sparky.

Mr. Upalupagus, strolling along in the general direction of Paris, turned, and grinned at them while he held up his trunk to stop the racket. "I know a secret," he said. That got everyone's attention.

Who doesn't want to know a secret?

They all stopped and gathered round.

"I need a secret right about now," said Sparky. "I feel bad and don't know what to do."

"First thing is to get calm because we can't think properly when we're upset, so this secret will help, Sparky," said Mr. Upalupagus.

"What's the secret?" Mr. King Cobra with no fangs asked as he slithered off of Mama Llama and onto Mr. Upalupagus. Round and round, he went, winding himself upwards on Mr. Upalupagus's trunk until he could look at Mr. Upalupagus straight in the eyes.

"Your breath is a secret," he announced, flapping his ears in joy.

"That's a secret?" asked Minnie the Hippo, blowing her breath into the air, trying to figure out how *that* could be a secret. It went in. It went out. Repeat.

"Minnie, come and help us, would you please?" Mr. Upalupagus coaxed. "You are always so willing," he added.

Minnie tried, and failed, to hide her smile as she lumbered over to Mr. Upalupagus, delicately holding a flower up for Mr. Upalupagus to smell.

"Spend a minute focusing on your breath. In and out. In and out," invited Mr. Upalupagus.

"This secret is also magic," Mr. Upalupagus said, piquing the interest of every single animal in attendance.

"Is it like pulling a bunny out of a hat, or making someone disappear?" asked Mr. Zebra, who didn't usually like to talk too much, but at the first sign of magic, he forgot all about not talking. Magic was at least as interesting as Bitcoin. Maybe.

Mr. Upalupagus laughed and said, "Yes, it's that kind of magic. It makes inside upsets disappear. And then you go from feeling unhappy to feeling happy. Like a see-through happy bubble floating light as a sunbeam through the air."

"Will my upset go away, Mr. Upalupagus?" asked Sparky the Dragon.

"Yes. What does this upset feel like, Sparky?"

"Like I want to hide. I'm sad and kind of worried," replied Sparky.

Zuzu the Cow said, "I know! I know! Upsets feel like a big, unhappy face in my head."

Marshmallow the Giraffe grinned and joined in, "Cross, crabby, cranky, and complaining."

Jessica the Dolphin couldn't resist. "Touchy, testy, troubled, tant ... trum ... yyyyyy," she said and then giggled.

Glitter the Seahorse, hovering in her bubble above Uni the Unicorn, sang out, "Sulky and snappy."

Uni grinned and hollered, "Snarly!"

Minnie the Hippo added, "Uneasy," and then thought of another one and hollered at the top of very big lungs, "Uncomfortable!"

"_____ [name of an upset feeling] feels awful, said, _____." [name of your child's animal].

Buster Beats, the DJ Gorilla, said, "When I feel upset, I don't do nice things." That realization put a frown on his face.

Uni the Unicorn, who was doing a handstand only it was a horn stand, said, "Me, too."

Jessica the Dolphin did a back walkover and announced, "Upsets feel like the opposite of playing."

Zuzu laughed at the antics of the Crew. "Moo-haha, it's fun to say those upset words, but it's not fun to feel them."

Mr. Upalupagus smiled fondly at Zuzu.

Of course, Mr. Upalupagus smiled fondly at everyone and everything, so that wasn't unusual. What was unusual was that he never seemed to get upset, so he must know some pretty important secrets.

"An inside upset is when you feel sad or mad or grumpy or fidgety, or any of those kinds of feelings that don't make you feel good … they don't feel natural. A happy bubble is when the upset disappears, and everything feels just right inside, like the sun came out and is shining inside of you."

Sparky the Dragon, fire-breathed the word "natural" into the sky.

"It's magic if you feel upset in one moment and then feel happy and like playing in the next."

They thought about that for a minute and nodded. Not one of them liked to be upset or stay that way. It just got in the way of … everything.

"Just breathe in and then out. You know how to do that, but do you know how to pay attention to breathing?"

"That's silly," said Happy the Dog. "That happens by itself," he added. "See," he said while he stood there breathing, his eyes crossed, staring at his nose!

"But here's a secret: If you pay attention to your breath, really close attention, you stop thinking upsetting thoughts," said Mr. Upalupagus.

"Sometimes I think bad things about the other animals. I don't like how that feels," said Mr. Bear.

Hawk brought his head out from under his wing and said, "I feel bad when I have bad thoughts about myself."

Glitter the Seahorse said, "I feel bad when I get huffy."

The animals started thinking about upsets and thoughts and feelings that felt bad. Nobody wanted to feel those.

Mama Llama stopped her Zoom meeting and joined the secret secrets meeting—after all, magic was pretty interesting.

Jessica the Dolphin stopped doing back walkovers and skipped over to plop down underneath Mr. Upalupagus.

Daisy the Pony stopped trotting in circles and grinned at Mr. Upalupagus, "Upsets are upsetting."

"Exactly right," said Mr. Upalupagus.

Ms. Gazelle stopped leaping and plopped down beside Mr. Upalupagus. She needed a rest. All this leaping was exhausting.

Mr. Upalupagus invited the Crew to try the secret, "Let's do it and see what happens. Close your eyes and take a breath and keep your attention on your breath as it goes into your body, and keep your attention as the breath goes out of your body."

"And a P.S. to this secret is from the yogis in the Eastern cultures: They say if you breathe deep and slow down the breathing, you live longer!"

Glitter glittered everyone, "Yay, that means there's more time to have fun if we live longer!"

With that good bit of news for animals who loved life, they did as he asked and felt themselves stop thinking; and if there were any bad feelings, they stopped too!

"Hmmmmm," said Hawk, "The bad thoughts are gone," he said in amazement. "And I feel joyful and harmless." Then he added, "I like it."

They all tried it and found that unhappy thoughts, upsetting thoughts, thoughts that criticized someone, cranky thoughts, sad thoughts, mad feelings … all of them disappeared—as long as they stay focused on the breath going in and the breath going out.

Mr. Upalupagus said, "See, your breath is magic. It makes upsets disappear—and now you know another secret."

"If you practice this secret every time you feel an upset, the upset will disappear. I promise. But you have to do it to see the magic work."

"I can do it, I can do it, I can do it too!" announced _____ [name of your child's animal] the _____ [type of animal].

"Sparky, do you feel better?" asked Mr. Upalupagus.

"Yes, I feel calm, and I don't feel confused," replied Sparky.

"It's hard to think clearly when we're upset. That's a good reason to clear up upsets right away when they appear."

Sparky dug up the scorched earth, added some seedling trees and some water, patted the earth around the roots, and smiled at the Crew. Problem solved!

After a few days and lots of practice watching their breath every time there was an upset, like when Ms. Gazelle caused a dust storm, and Mr.

Bear growled at Mr. Upalupagus, they finally arrived in Paris, feeling free as the breeze!

The first place they wanted to see was the Eiffel Tower because it was one of the most famous towers in the world.

Mr. Upalupagus was so taken with it that he didn't pay any attention to where he was moving, when he moved his considerable bulk the wrong way and felt a bump. Oh, oh, the tower did what he really hoped it wouldn't and fell—all the way down.

"Oops," said Mr. Upalupagus. "Bless me."

"Bless you?" repeated Glitter "You didn't sneeze; you knocked over one of the most famous towers in the whole wide world, Mr. Upalupagus!"

But then, Ms. Gazelle, feeling so grateful for everything Mr. Upalupagus did for them, said, "It's okay, Mr. Upalupagus, we'll find a way to fix this!"

"I know a secret," Mr. Upalupagus announced.

"Are you sure now is the best time to talk about secrets?" asked Happy the Dog.

"Now is a great time, Happy. The secret secret is called Blessing Mistakes," Mr. Upalupagus replied.

"It was a mistake and being upset about a mistake never helps. It's not natural to get upset over a mistake. We make quite a few of them. In fact, they come along as part of every day, as you've noticed, and if we give the one who made a mistake Grace (that means be nice or kind to them) instead of grief (that means be upset with them or mean to them), everyone feels good."

"Mistakes are not good," said Mr. Bear.

"Did you make a mistake today, Mr. Bear?" Mr. Upalupagus asked.

"No, and I didn't make one yesterday or the day before either," he answered, poking his massive head straight out at Mr. Upalupagus, giving him a defiant look.

"Then you needn't worry, had you, Mr. Bear?" said Mr. Upalupagus.

Mr. Zebra, having quietly contemplated what Mr. Upalupagus shared, said, "I made a mistake. I argued with Sparky the Dragon about which direction we should go even though she was flying so high she could see which way to go. I thought I was right, and I wasn't."

Mr. Upalupagus drew Mr. Zebra close and gave him a big hug and said, "Bless you, Mr. Zebra. You matter more than the mistake."

Mr. Zebra didn't know what to make of Mr. Upalupagus's idea of blessing a mistake, but he felt really good inside of himself because he didn't get into trouble for his mistake.

He got a hug instead.

This was a cool secret.

"Are you sure you should 'bless' a mistake', Mr. Upalupagus?" Daisy the Pony asked.

"Of course, Daisy. We all make mistakes no matter how hard we try not to."

Mr. Bear lowered his head. He no longer looked threatening "I, I," he stuttered, "I do make mistakes. Lots of them, but I don't want you to think I'm bad."

"Bless every one of your mistakes, Mr. Bear," said Mr. Upalupagus kindly. "You matter more than your mistakes," he said.

Mr. Bear thought about that, blessed himself for making the mistake of saying he didn't make mistakes, and said out loud, "I matter more than the mistake." He danced a little bear-jig, which looked more like a galumphing lurching jump, but he didn't mind; it came naturally to him!

That caused the whole crew to do the same, and as usual, chaos reigned for a few minutes in the form of dancing, and limbs flying and flailing everywhere—sometimes into each other.

Mama Llama ambled over and after thinking deeply about this secret, said, "I don't feel good inside when I give someone grief instead of Grace when they make a mistake. I'm happy to learn this secret."

No more worrying about mistakes—ever!

"The next part of this secret about blessing a mistake, is to make it right. I caused the tower to fall, so I must make that right," said Mr. Upalupagus.

He raised his trunk into the air and let out the loudest elephant cry ever. *Hhhnnnn!* It could be heard all over the city, even by King Cobra with no fangs who had no ears but felt the vibration!

The elephants from the Paris Zoo came stampeding, and the ants came marching, one by one to help put the tower back up, and before long, it was back where it belonged.

King Cobra grinned and slithered alongside the marching ants, pretending to march himself, which was quite hard since he was a snake who slithered.

It even felt right to make it right. That was good news.

Mr. Upalupagus explained that it is hard for a few seconds but that it's so good after you apologize, because you feel so much better. If you don't apologize, you stay upset. That's no fun!

Wow! That was a secret itself. It felt better to make a mistake right than to pretend it didn't happen, which caused an uncomfortable feeling.

Mr. Zebra, remembering the part about "making it right," apologized to Sparky for his mistake.

Sparky, having caught on to this whole blessing mistakes thing to make everyone feel as good as when they watched his fire, said, "You matter more than the mistake, Mr. Zebra."

Glitter glittered everyone because happy is easy and fun to spread!

Just then, Ms. Gazelle spotted a mobile crepe stand and darted off, her mouth already watering. *The French sure know how to cook,* she thought. Some of the crepes had cheese and lettuce and other yummy green stuff, and some had berries and cream that Happy the Dog and Marshmallow got all over their happy faces.

That reminded Sparky, Daisy, Jessica, and Mr. Bear that they wanted to go face painting.

And that reminded Mama Llama that she wanted to go see the Louvre to see famous paintings.

And that reminded Hawk, Minnie, and Marshmallow that they wanted to have tea and croissants at a sidewalk café.

And that reminded Glitter, Uni, Mr. King Cobra with no fangs, and Zuzu that they wanted to go to Disneyland Paris.

And that reminded Buster Beats, the DJ Gorilla, that he wanted to do a street-side performance of "The Boss's" best.

And they all ran off feeling lighter than air; the secret secrets were working!

Sparky paused, turned to the sky, and breathed her fire into the words: Bless your mistakes!

The End

For Parents, Grandparents, Caregivers, for Anyone and Everyone: The Motley Crew in Paris!

The Breath Is a Big Secret
As taught by Eckhart Tolle, put your full attention on the intake breath and then on the outward breath. Repeat several times. Notice you can't think or have bad feelings and focus on the breath at the same time, and this leads to calmness. This is called, "taking a conscious breath." Do this when you feel an upset coming on. You can also do this as many times a day as you think of it: in lineups, at traffic lights, at work, anytime during the day.

Teach this to your children, telling them it's a secret not everyone knows! Invite your children to teach this to their teddy bears and share it with their friends to use when there is an upset.

Blessing Mistakes
Learning to give others and ourselves Grace instead of grief when a mistake is made. Mistakes are normal. Learn from them, make them right, and then let them go.

Getting upset about a mistake is stressful. Stress is not good for us unless we're running away from something dangerous.

Mistakes and success coexist. We often do something wrong a few times before we do it right.

When your child makes a mistake, say, "Bless you. It's really all right to make a mistake." Use words that make you feel good when you say them. Another example is, "You matter more than the mistake."

Remember that we don't want to devalue anyone when he or she makes a mistake.

When you make a mistake, say to yourself, "I matter more than the mistake." Then make it right.

By blessing a mistake, giving others Grace instead of grief, everyone feels better. The one who made the mistake doesn't have to feel bad, and the one blessing the mistake feels good because he or she is being kind instead of mean.

Take corrective action and responsibility for the mistake. We feel better when we make it right.

> If you hurt someone by making a rude, mean, or criticizing remark, apologize.
> If you spilled something, wipe it up.
> If you lied, apologize, and tell the truth.
> If you broke something, replace it, or pay for it.
> Ask the other person how you can make it right, and do it if you can.

CHAPTER 6

Teaching Kids How to Release Anger with Mr. Upalupagus's Secret Secrets

Note to parents and caregivers: Invite your children or your family as a whole to participate where indicated, or at any time during the stories!

D(Anger)

Doodle the Duck, whose beak was turned down in a frown—slowly pointed it up, way up at Bruce the Moose, who was backing away from the mighty and mad little duck.

"You stole my lunch," quacked Doodle, flapping his wings full force at Bruce the Moose.

"I did not," Bruce the Moose harrumphed and came to a stop.

"Did too."

"Did not."

The Crew who was watching in various stages of disbelief and concern, sighed with relief when Mr. Upalupagus ambled over.

"I know a secret," said Mr. Upalupagus.

That got everyone's attention, as it always did.

Doodle Duck and Bruce the Moose momentarily dropped most of their "mad" and turned toward Mr. Upalupagus.

Everyone loves secrets.

"Anger is one letter away from danger."

He picked up a stick with his trunk and spelled it out in the sand.

(D)anger.

"We're dangerous to ourselves and others when we're angry."

"How so, Mr. Upalupagus?" asked Glitter the Seahorse.

"Sometimes angry people hit others. That's dangerous."

"Being angry is like poisoning yourself," he continued. "That's also dangerous to our own bodies."

"Huh!" cried King Cobra with no fangs. That was an alarming thought. He liked his slithery, scaly, shiny body and did not want to poison it.

"Ada mea Mr. Up, up neeee awayyyyyyy?" asked Minnie the Hippo, bringing a flower she'd just picked over for him to smell. Although she had to repeat herself in English that could be understood because she spoke in her made-up language. "How is anger dangerous to our bodies, Mr. Upalupagus?"

"It means that when we are angry, our bodies make "I'm stressed" chemicals, and that hurts our insides. They don't work as good when they are bombarded with anger. Just like we don't do things very well when we're angry."

"That's a good reason to stop being angry," said Mr. Zebra. He'd rather not talk, but he especially liked it when things were reasonable, and this seemed reasonable.

"How do we stop being angry?" asked Sparky the Dragon as she swooped down, breathing fantastic-looking fire on the way.

That momentarily stopped them all as they gazed at the beautiful fire racing through the sky.

"One way is to go look at yourself in the mirror when you're angry," Mr. Upalupagus said.

Mr. Zebra raised one eyebrow into a big question mark.

"When you were looking at each other when you were angry, Doodle and Bruce, what did you see?"

"Um, a-not-very-nice-to-look-at face," Bruce said.

That offended Doodle, who stomped his webbed foot and said, "That's rude!"

"Doodle, what does it feel like inside of yourself when you stomp your feet?" Mr. Upalupagus asked.

"It feels bad," he quacked.

"It's important to notice when we're angry, we don't feel natural," said Mr. Upalupagus. "That tells us that anger isn't natural."

"And what did you see, Doodle, when you looked at Bruce the Moose?" he continued.

Doodle paused, realizing he saw that same thing on Bruce's face as must have been on his own. Anger didn't look very good on anyone's face, and he told Mr. Upalupagus so.

The conversation was starting to take the oomph out of the anger Doodle Duck and Bruce the Moose were feeling, and they mostly forgot the rest of their anger in favor of curiosity *about* their anger.

That felt better.

"But Mr. Upalupagus, I'm right when I'm angry," said Happy the Dog, who had been happily chasing his tail.

The Crew thought about that and nodded in agreement.

"Yes, we are sure we're right, but we're never right when we're angry," Mr. Upalupagus added. "We're just angry, trying to prove we're right."

Marshmallow the Giraffe leaned down to whisper in Mr. Upalupagus's ear, "Can't I be right and angry at the same time?" Since Marshmallow's whisper was like her outside voice, everyone heard.

"We can be right without being angry. But we can't be angry without thinking we are right," said Mr. Upalupagus.

"If anger is danger, and it is, can it ever be right?" Mr. Upalupagus asked.

There was a lot to ponder in this secret.

"Iknow, Iknow, Iknowone, too, Mr. Upalupagus," cried Jessica the Dolphin, each word connected to the next with hardly a breath in between, "When I'm angry I'm just telling the truth."

Mr. Upalupagus smiled and said, "Every time we get angry, we think we're being honest. Really, we're just blaming, and that's not honest; that's just blaming."

Mama Llama, after deeply considering this issue, announced, "Every time we get angry, we think we're important."

"Ugh," said Hawk. "That's true," and stuck his head back under his wing.

Mr. Bear who'd been yumming up some honey from a honeycomb, said, "People who are angry are scary."

Zuzu the Cow said, "I don't like being around them."

Georgia the Horse said, "They're no fun."

Hawk brought his head out from under his wing again. He is usually thinking pretty hard when that's where his head is. He said, "I think I'm strong when I'm angry, but I shake when I'm angry. That doesn't seem strong."

"Very wise," said Mr. Upalupagus. "Are you sure you're not an owl instead of a hawk?" Mr. Upalupagus teased.

"Anger is a weakness," stated Daisy, clapping her hooves with her awareness.

"Anger is weakness?" asked Uni the Unicorn.

"Yes, Daisy's right," replied Mr. Upalupagus.

"Anyone who is angry is 'bluffing you and is using hysteria in place of intelligence,' as once taught by a wise man named Mr. Howard," added Mr. Upalupagus. "That's an important secret!"

"What's hysteria?" asked Glitter.

"Acting like a loud nut," answered Mr. Upalupagus.

Then Mr. Upalupagus made a statement that changed the way they thought about anger and power or strength.

"True power is peaceful." Like when we bless a mistake—we have the power to end an upset and that's peaceful.

"True peace is powerful." Like when we look inside instead of blaming someone—it's powerful because we feel peaceful.

"Those are important secret secrets," said Mr. Upalupagus.

"Anger isn't peaceful or powerful. Don't be fooled by it."

Anger wasn't any of the things they thought.

"Anger doesn't just poison our body; it poisons our thinking, our feelings, and our actions," added Mr. Upalupagus.

"How do you or others act when you're angry?" Mr. Upalupagus asked the Crew.

"Bad-tempered," grinned Buster Beats, the DJ Gorilla, who was really good-tempered most of the time, which was why he was grinning when he answered the question.

"Bullying," Ms. Gazelle said, folding her knees to the ground for a much-needed rest from her restless circling.

"Confrontational," said Doodle the Duck. "I want to fight when I'm mad."

"Cranky," Bruce the Moose added.

"Cross," said Fluffles the Hamster.

"Fuming," Jack-A-Lena the Jack Russell declared.

"Furious," Levilian the Lion pronounced.

"Grouchy," Beninsula the Beagle declared.

"Grumpy," Georgia the Horse stated.

"Hateful," Zippa the Monkey shouted.

"Hostile," Taloola the Owl exclaimed.

"Huffy," Cheddar the Mouse proclaimed.

"Impatient," Wally the Wombat uttered.

"Insulting," confirmed Daisy the Pony.

"Irritable," Rosehips the Reindeer stated.

"Mad," Lexi the Sloth asserted.

"Offensive," Stella the Phoenix pointed out.

"Ornery," stated Great Grampa, the Steady Ox, who was hardly ever that. But even the most wonderful animals have to work on themselves sometimes, and if he got ornery, he had a good talk with himself about his "wrong thinking"! That turned him into a wonderful animal that no one could resist (and everyone could love—well, almost everyone)!

"Outraged, punishing, pushy and rude," said [your child's or family's animal] _____.

"Raging," said Minnie, although she'd never done that yet.

"Spoiling for a fight," said Leo the Lion.

"Testy," said Sapphire the White Siberian Tiger.

"Threatening," said Lexi the Sloth.

"Touchy," said Stella the Phoenix.

"Mean," said Ms. Gazelle.

"Temper-tantrumy, trumer," said Doodle. He loved to play with words, words being one of his favorite things.

"I bite," said King Cobra with no fangs.

The Crew shivered. They didn't want a bite, even though Mr. King Cobra had no fangs.

"I run and hide," said Georgia the Horse, which was a challenge with her pet llama lying under her, and the barn cat hitching a ride on her rear!

"Anger doesn't feel good," said Lexi the Sloth.

"Are there more ways to get anger out of us other than running to look at our angry faces in the mirror?" asked Taloola the Owl.

"Can we have an operation and get it out?" Wally the Wombat wondered out loud.

"Can we promise never to feel it again? Will that work?" asked Beninsula the Beagle.

"Can we give it heck when it appears?" Uni the Unicorn asked.

"Can we hit ... Maybe not," suggested Jessica the Dolphin.

The Crew laughed, giggled, sniggered, snickered, hooted, snorted, cackled, chortled, guffawed, and tittered!

"You can't use anger to get rid of anger," said Mr. Upi.

"Can we hide from it?" Zuzu the Cow wondered.

"Can we tell it to go away?" Marshmallow the Giraffe inquired.

"Can we trick it?" Glitter the Seahorse questioned. She'd been silently considering this secret because she didn't like the angry feeling and wanted more than anything to get rid of it.

"We can watch it, like watching it from behind the scenes, like it's going on a stage, and we watch it from behind the stage," offered Mr. Upalupagus.

"That sounds crazy," said Happy, and they all agreed.

"What's crazy is to act out anger. Watching it takes its power from it," explained Mr. Upalupagus. "That's another secret!"

"Still sounds crazy," said Georgia the Horse.

"Let's try it right now. Think of something that makes you angry."

He paused so everyone could think of something that made them angry.

The Crew shouted out, over each other, as usual!

"When someone takes the last cookie," said Jack-A-Lena the Jack Russell.

"When someone disagrees with me," said Levilian the Lion.

"When someone tells me what to do," said Zippa the Monkey.

"When someone leaves me out," said Cheddar the Mouse.

"When I don't get to do what I want," said Minnie the Hippo.

"When another bear runs in front of me, cutting me off," said Mr. Bear.

"When somebody doesn't do what they should do!" said Mama Llama.

"Feel the anger. Now pretend you're at a concert on the stage. Leave this angry you on the stage and take the curious you and step behind the stage and watch the anger as it acts out on the stage. Watch what the anger says and does," invited Mr. Upalupagus.

"That's what you look like when you're angry."

They did as he asked, and each and every one felt the anger they'd been feeling disappear. In its place appeared some deep awarenesses about anger.

"Wow," Doodle the Duck cried. "That's so awesome to be able to get rid of anger like that."

Mr. Upalupagus said, "I know another secret."

They were all ears, beaks, snouts, hooters, schnozzles, muzzles …

"We can remind ourselves we don't need this angry story anymore," said Mr. Upalupagus. "Keep a note in your pocket and pull it out and read it to remind yourself that you don't need to be angry. That it's not helpful in any way," he finished.

"I know one that I do," said Mr. Zebra. "I take myself out for a walk in nature to work it out. Nature helps me do that."

"Yes, nature helps us find our own nature, Mr. Zebra," said Mr. Upalupagus. "That's a good secret."

"This is a big deal. There's lots of anger in the world," said Cheddar the Mouse.

"Yes, there's so much more for us to learn to dissolve our anger," replied Mr. Upalupagus, "that it's to be continued."

The End

For Parents, grandparents, caregivers, for anyone and everyone:
(D)Anger

Lesson: Getting Rid Of (D)anger

For the parent:

To release anger, read each word separately. Close your eyes, and let the word bring up any feelings, images, or physical sensations they do, and say while you feel it, "I'm so sorry I'm attached to/identified with

_____." This simple strategy dissolves anger. Before we can be calm and rational as a natural response, we need to rid ourselves of anger.

The Word List

Abrupt, admonishing, affronted, aflame, aggravated, aggressive, angry, annoyed, antagonistic, apoplectic, argumentative, awful, bad-tempered, badgering, belligerent, beside myself, blazing, blistering, blustering, bothered, boiling, brusque, brutal, bullying, burning, cantankerous, castigating, censuring, chastising, cheesed off, cold, complaining, confrontational, contentious, crabby, cranky, critical, cross, cruel, curt, dangerous, defensive, defiant, demanding, difficult, disapproving, disciplining discontent, disgruntled, displeased, disrespectful, dissatisfied, disturbed, edgy, enraged, exasperated, exasperating, explosive, fanatical, ferocious, fiery, foul, fractious, frenzied, frothing, fuming, furious, gnashing, goading, getting on my nerves, grouchy, grumpy, gunning (for someone), harsh, hassling, hateful, heated, hopping mad, hostile, hot-headed, hounding, huffy, impatient, impudent, incensed, inciting, indignant, infuriated, insistent, insolent, insulting, intolerant, ire, irking, irritable, irritated, livid, mad, maddened, moody, narrow-minded, objecting, offended, offensive, opinionated, ornery, out of sorts, outraged, passive-aggressive, peevish, penalizing, petulant, piqued, prejudiced, prickly, provoked, pugnacious, punishing, punitive, pushy, put out, quarrelsome, rabid, raging, reactive, rebuking, rejecting, relentless, reprimanding, reproving, resentful, rigid, riled, rude, ruthless, sadistic, scalding, scorching, searing, seething, severe, sharp, short-tempered, slighting, smoldering, snappy, snippy, spitting mad, spoiling (for a fight), stern, stinging, strict, surly, teed off, temper tantrum, terrible, terse, testy, threatening, ticked off, touchy, truculent, uncompromising, unrelenting, up in arms, vehement, vexed, vexing, violent, worked up, wound up, wrathful.

Anger Poisons Us
As Sadhguru teaches and science confirms, anger causes poisonous chemicals to be made in our bodies. When we get angry it's a good idea to remind ourselves that we are literally poisoning our bodies. Research it to learn more.

Me in the Mirror
Go look in the mirror in the middle of a big mad. If you have lost your mad by the time you get there, make a mad face on purpose, and look at yourself.

The Bluff
Vernon Howard teaches us that anyone who is angry is trying to bluff us into believing he or she is intelligent. Teach your children that anger is not intelligent; it's the opposite.

Tense and Calm
Invite your children to feel how tense they are when they're angry and how calm they feel after the anger passes.

The Watcher
Watch the anger instead of being dragged away by it. Pretend there are two of you, and one of you stays on the "stage" and carries on in an angry way. The other stands behind the stage, curiously watching the angry you. We don't want to be that anymore.

My Angry Story
As John de Ruiter teaches, put a note in your pocket that says, "I don't need my raging story anymore." Pull it out and look at it every time anger arises.

My Time Out
Take yourself away from the others. Go outside and do something physical instead of acting the anger out.

Anger: The Hanger-on-er

Note to parents and caregivers: Invite your children or your family as a whole to participate where indicated, or at any time during the stories!

The Crew was on its way to South Africa. Mr. Upalupagus said he had a special secret secret in store for them. On the way they just had to go to a wildlife park because, well, most of them *were* wildlife!

They made many friends to play with on safari at Kruger National Park and posed for the tourists like the hams they were.

Anger came and went as they practiced the secrets they had learned on their last trip. It was pretty cool to go from angry to awesome in a couple of heartbeats!

But Doodle the Duck and Bruce the Moose were at it again. Doodle just couldn't let go of Bruce the Moose helping himself to Doodle's lunch, even though he tried every anger-releasing technique Mr. Upalupagus had taught them. The anger went away, but then it came back when he thought about his lunch.

Sometimes anger hangs on and comes back, but we can always get rid of it *each time* it appears.

They were faced off like a pair of cranky buffalos, only Doodle was tiny and Bruce the Moose … wasn't. So, they looked kind of funny even though anger is *never* funny.

A few of the animals scurried close to Mr. Upalupagus, hoping he'd pull a secret out of his trunk ASAP.

"I know a secret," he said.

Right on time!

The Crew, except for Doodle and Bruce, were so happy about that they jumped, leapt, soared, hurdled, bounced, hopped, sprang, and vaulted with joy—another secret to make them feel really good inside of themselves. Just what they needed.

There was nothing better, really.

Maybe ice cream?

Nope, there was nothing better than feeling good inside, no matter what was going on outside. The bliss barometer on high was better than anything!

"We can say to ourselves, 'Anger, you're not the boss of me,' and take some deep, slow breaths."

They were beginning to understand that anger could be shooed away before it made them miserable—and do and say dumb things.

Doodle and Bruce grumbled but tried it because they didn't want to feel how they were feeling.

"Anger you're not the boss of me," quacked Doodle, and then he cried real tears because once the anger let go of him, relief came.

That tugged at Bruce the Moose's heart, and his anger just disappeared all on its own. So, he lifted Doodle up using his beautiful rack of horns and cuddled Doodle as best as he could with a rack of horns!

Mr. Upalupagus wasn't done, though, because anger sure did ruin a lot of animals' fun times.

"Here's another secret," announced Mr. Upalupagus.

"We can put our hands over our hearts."

Which they all did immediately!

"And get in touch with the kindness in our hearts."

"It works," announced Bruce. "It just happened to me! My heart started doing my thinking for me, and my anger went away."

"I know another way to get rid of anger," he hollered. "We can run around outside and burn off the anger," said Bruce, who immediately galloped in a circle around the Crew, forgetting Doodle was on board. Doodle clasped his feet around Bruce's horn and hung on for the ride, his body swinging out and around and up and down!

That started all the animals running and galumphing and slithering as fast as they could to see how it felt, just for the fun of it! And they thought the practice would be good, because if anger did get the best of them, *they were going to get the best of it*!

When they settled down, Doodle righted himself on Bruce's horns and asked, "Could I stomp on the ground to get rid of my anger?"

"If you must, but then you also have to tell everyone around you that this is 100 percent your problem, and you're working on it. It has nothing to do with anyone or anything else."

"Huh?" said Doodle. "Bruce the Moose stole my lunch, so my anger is about him." That made Doodle angry all over again, and he flew to the ground in a giant swoop.

"No, if you have anger come up in you, it was already there before whatever happened," explained Mr. Upalupagus. The he continued, "Otherwise, the incident would run off of you like water off of a duck's back."

Doodle the Duck grinned at that, being a duck, and all.

"That's another secret," said Mr. Upalupagus. "All the feelings we have are already inside of us even though we say they were caused by something or someone outside of us. How else could we feel the feelings if they weren't already there? Do you think the other animal *put* the feelings we are feeling inside of us?"

"Hmmmmm," said Mama Llama. "That's a good point."

"What else could I have done?" asked Doodle. "I was hungry, you know," he finished, feeling a bit defensive again.

"You could ask him if he took your lunch. You could talk to him about it without accusing or blaming him. The important thing is how you feel inside. You don't want to be angry about it. It's not good for your digestion."

Doodle thought about that and nodded his head.

"Can anyone see a good reason for anger?" Mr. Upalupagus said.

"No," said Sparky the Dragon. Then she blew the words, "Say no to anger," into the sky.

They all had to pause for that event. Sparky's fire was so amazing.

"Nope," pitched in Mr. King Cobra with no fangs.

They all chimed in.

"Ummmmm, welllllll, hmmmmmm, no, I guess not," said [insert your child's/family's animal].

"I can't really see one," mused Glitter the Seahorse.

"No, there doesn't seem to be a good reason to be angry," said Minnie the Hippo.

"Good to notice," said Mr. Upalupagus.

"I know another secret," he added.

The Crew cheered and bounced up and down!

"Did you notice that when someone is angry, they're not rational, they don't make sense, they're not reasonable?" added Mr. Upalupagus.

"Yah, I'm like that. I don't make sense when I'm angry. I say stup … I mean I say not-smart things," said King Cobra with no fangs.

"Anger is not our friend," said Mr. Upalupagus.

They all agreed.

Bruce the Moose hung his head, his beautiful horns almost touching the ground.

"I'm sorry that I took your lunch, Doodle."

Doodle the Duck's anger disappeared, and he asked, "Were you hungry?"

"Yes. I'm always hungry. I'm pretty big, and I need a lot to eat. But I shouldn't have taken your lunch."

"Bless you, Bruce the Moose. You matter more than the mistake," said Doodle, beaming now.

"Wow," he said, "that felt so much better than the anger felt." Then he added, "I couldn't bless a mistake when I was angry."

"Yes, it's important to get rid of our anger," smiled Mr. Upalupagus. "It's easier to be kind when we're not angry."

Doodle looked at Bruce and said, "I would have shared with you if you told me."

"Me two," said [insert your child's/family's animal].

"Me, three," said Marshmallow the Giraffe.

"Me, four," mooed Zuzu the Cow.

"Me five," added Uni the Unicorn.

"Me six," announced Jessica the Dolphin.

"Me, seven," agreed Wally the Wombat.

"Me, eight," said Glitter, and glittered everyone!

And on and on they went until each animal said they would have shared with Bruce the Moose.

Every. Single. One. Of. Them.

That's because it's natural to share, and they liked feeling natural.

"Really?" he asked, his head slowly lifting.

"Of course," they said, some of them whispering, some of them shouting, and some of them at all decibels in between.

But then …

Anger being so familiar …

Doodle asked, "Shouldn't Bruce the Moose be punished for stealing my lunch?" He sent an apologetic look at Bruce, but he wanted to know. "How will he learn?"

"We'll see," Mr. Upalupagus said mysteriously.

After a long trip through grasslands and plains, they arrived at a remote village in South Africa. The lions and tigers and zebras and gorillas and monkeys were in a circle. In the center of the circle stood a chimpanzee.

As the Crew got closer, they began to hear what was being said—and it was all good things about the chimp. A smile was forming on his little face.

"This is called Ubuntu," explained Mr. Upalupagus. "We learned about it before, but I wanted you to see it firsthand. It's quite remarkable." He paused to give them time to remember using this way to help others.

"To think and act this way helps people remember that they are naturally good; we sometimes have to remind them after they've made a mistake or acted out!"

Everyone in the Ubuntu circle was smiling, and you could feel the love and joy radiate from each and every animal, especially the chimp in the middle of the circle. He told his village that he knew that he made a mistake and thanked them so much for loving him the way they did, and that he would work really hard at staying in his good nature! After all, he had good incentive—his village loved him!

"Gather round in a circle, and Bruce the Moose, can you go to the center of it, please?" Mr. Upalupagus kindly invited him.

The animals shuffled, slithered, galloped, ran, hoped, swooped, and inched into a circle.

Bruce the Moose felt a bit scared even though Mr. Upalupagus didn't have a mean bone in his over-three-hundred of them. And he'd just witnessed people showing love and praising the chimp who had taken a banana that wasn't his. Still, he felt a bit nervous.

Mr. Upalupagus hugged him and nudged him into the center of the circle, reassuring him with trunk-cuddles all the way.

"Everyone, please tell Bruce the Moose everything you love about him … like about him … and tell him why you love having him here in our Crew," said Mr. Upalupagus.

For an hour, they stood together and told Bruce the Moose all about what a wonderful animal he was.

"You often go ahead of us and make sure we're safe," said Taloola the Owl.

"You stop to help us when we're looking for food," announced Lexi the Sloth.

"You were kind to me when I felt bad the other day," mentioned Levilian the Lion.

"You used your antlers to get me out of the mud when I got stuck," said Beninsula the Beagle, blowing Bruce a kiss.

Bruce the Moose got the message. He was loved even though he made a mistake.

Bruce looked at Doodle Duck and said, "How can I make this right, Doodle?" His head now held high.

Doodle said, "Maybe you could help me pick up the garbage on the beach next week. People eat and then throw their wrappers away and it's a mess."

"Yes," Bruce the Moose cried, "I'd love to do that. My horns can pick up a lot of garbage!" He paused for a minute and then added, "Will there be food?"

The Crew laughed. Bruce the Moose did think about his stomach quite a bit. Quite a few others could relate.

They were all so curious about this way of living where there was no punishment, so they sought out the animals they'd just witnessed for an explanation of Ubuntu.

The chimp, who had just received the blessing of Ubuntu from his tribe said, "This makes me feel like taking more care about how I act. They just showed me how much they love me and how much faith they have in me. That feels so good."

The rhino said, "When we do this, the one who make the mistake feels more like making it right."

"So, I climbed a tree and got a banana and returned the one I took. While I was there, I got some for everyone in the village!" said the chimp.

"This method is like Blessing Mistakes and helps everyone connect with their True Nature. The one made the mistake and the ones who are encouraging them," said Mr. Upalup.

The rhino added, "Our tribes have learned, over thousands of years, that unity and affirming each other has more power to change behavior than shame and punishment does."

The chimp said, "It's more kind than angry punishing is."

They thanked the tribe members and went off to think.

"Will anger disappear now?" asked Doodle.

"Not completely, not right away; it will take some time. But it will have less and less of a hold on us as we practice all the secret secrets."

"The last time I was mad, many years ago, I was mad for one minute, and then it went away, and I felt joyful inside," said Mr. Upalupagus.

"Really? Practice like practicing for a tennis match?" asked Mama Llama.

"Exactly like that," said Mr. Upalupagus with a fond look for Mama Llama. He loved giving fond looks, so he gave one to each of his wonderful Crew, who, he knew, would get a lot of practice practicing.

And they did … sooner rather than later. Hawk flew too close to Glitter, startling her. Glitter pinched Minnie. There were a lot of opportunities to practice getting rid of anger.

Of course, they couldn't leave South Africa without traveling to Cape Town, on the very tip of the continent!

And that meant they had to go to Robben Island by boat to see where Nelson Mandela spent twenty-seven years in prison because he wanted black people to have the same rights as all people.

As they walked through his cell in the prison, Ms. Gazelle cried tears she just couldn't hold back. She hoped that everyone would do the work that Mr. Upalupagus was teaching so people could think clearly and could love freely—and make the world a better place so no one had to suffer. Life, in her view, was to be cherished, every single bit of it.

"Did Mr. Mandela get angry?" asked Bruce the Moose.

"Everyone does unless they're awakened to their True Nature, but some people learn sooner than others how to dissolve it every time it arises, so it doesn't ruin their lives and relationships."

Mr. Upalupagus continued, "He lived and taught nonviolence. You can't teach nonviolence if you're angry. I don't know how he felt for sure, but I know that if he had anger, he saw the uselessness of it! Just like we have!"

"We're all little Mr. Mandela's right now," said Minnie the Hippo. "Being peaceful!" she added.

The Crew nodded their heads and then broke into happy cheers because that's what was happening inside of them!

The End

For parents, grandparents, caregivers, for anyone and everyone: "Anger: The Hanger-on-er"

Lesson: Getting Rid of Anger

"Anger, you're not the boss of me!"
Teach your kids to tell the anger as soon as it appears, "You're not the boss of me."

Heart Anger Away
When anger arises, put your hand over your heart and see if you can connect with your essential, True Nature of kindness and dismiss the anger. Invite kids to think of their favorite places or favorite stuffy's, to help them get that good feeling. Adults can think of someone they love and keep that feeling as their baseline when anger arises.

If You Must
If you hit a pillow or kick the door, or stomp your feet, tell anyone who is watching that they are safe and that you don't know how to control your anger yet, but you are working on it. Apologize to them. Bless yourself for your mistake, making sure to make the mistake right.

Preexisting Feelings (Sadhguru and Guy Finley)

Teach your child that they've never experienced anything outside of themselves. All feelings are preexisting inside of us and are catalyzed by an event or another. We know that to be true because we feel the upsetting emotions *inside* of us. That's why sometimes we react and sometimes we don't. It all depends on which identity is operating us as to what upsetting thoughts and emotions will rise up from the unconscious where they are stored.

It's our job to self-regulate out of negativity and into our natural state.

Emotions Make Us Confused and Crazy (Eckhart Tolle)
Notice that you get confused and irrational when big emotions like anger arise. Eckhart Tolle teaches us that two things will happen when a big emotion arises. We will be upset, and then confusion will be felt. Then we will become irrational/crazy. We don't need those states anymore.

Use Blessing Mistakes
Use blessing mistakes: "You matter more than the mistake." Do this silently while the person is angry because saying it to them while they're angry might bring out more of their anger. But if you use it anyway, silently, *you* can feel better around angry people. Use it on yourself if you feel angry: "I matter more than my mistake of being angry," and then make your mistake right (apologize, etc.).

Ubuntu
Perform Ubuntu for someone who has made a mistake or has displayed bad behavior. You don't have to put them in a circle; you can have this conversation anywhere. Notice how it changes your relationship and deepens connection and trust. This is a humanitarian way to handle bad behavior. Be a humanitarian—start anew every moment.

The End

AFTERWORD

Thank you for considering that there is another way to live in the world and to handle mistakes in a less stressful and more supportive, connecting way.

There is nothing more important than real well-being for ourselves and for those we love. For that to come, we must find what stands in the way of well-being.

You just did.

SOCIAL MEDIA AND CONTACT INFORMATION

The Blessing Mistakes Movement

Please help us make this a worldwide movement by teaching everyone you know how to bless mistakes. There is a free download on www.thekidcode.ca under the *Resources* tab. You can also register to be a part of the movement on the website.

The blessing mistakes strategy comes from my book, *The Kid Code, 30 Second Parenting Strategies* available here:

Amazon.ca

Amazon.com

Barnes & Noble

To become a Kid Code teacher:
https://www.thekidcode.ca/become-a-kid-code-teacher

Take a class and get more information:
https://www.thekidcode.ca/take-a-kid-code-class

Facebook Page
The Kid Code, Brenda Miller (for parents to ask questions about their kids' problems and strategies to help them, including Blessing Mistakes).
https://www.facebook.com/thekidcode

Printed in the United States
by Baker & Taylor Publisher Services